EDITH

EDITH HAMILTON won a notable place in contemporary
American letters through her books on the culture of the
ancient world. A student of the classics from her earliest
youth, she read Latin and Greek all her life for her own
pleasure. She was graduated from Bryn Mawr in 1894 and
did graduate work in Greek and Latin at the University of
Munich, to which she was the first woman ever admitted.
She was for twenty-five years Head Mistress of the Bryn
Mawr School for Girls in Baltimore. It was not until 1930,
when she was 63, that she began her writing career with *The
Greek Way.* At once Miss Hamilton won a wide and ardent
audience. That audience was augmented with each of her sub-
sequent books: *The Roman Way, Spokesmen for God, Three
Greek Plays, Mythology, Witness to the Truth,* and *The
Echo of Greece.* All of these are published in paperback as
well as in cloth bindings. A collection of her essays entitled
The Ever-Present Past is also available in both cloth and
paper.

Miss Hamilton won the National Achievement Award
in 1950, received the honorary degrees of Doctor of Letters
from the University of Rochester and the University of
Pennsylvania, and was a member of the American Academy
of Arts and Letters. In 1957 she was made an honorary
citizen of Athens and was decorated with the Golden Cross
of the Order of Benefaction by King Paul of Greece.

BOOKS BY EDITH HAMILTON

THE GREEK WAY

THE ROMAN WAY

THREE GREEK PLAYS

WITNESS TO THE TRUTH

SPOKESMEN FOR GOD

THE ECHO OF GREECE

THE EVER-PRESENT PAST

EDITH HAMILTON

Spokesmen for God

THE GREAT TEACHERS
OF THE OLD TESTAMENT

❖ ❖ ❖ ❖ ❖ ❖ ❖ ❖ ❖ ❖ ❖ ❖ ❖ ❖ ❖ ❖ ❖ ❖ ❖ ❖

The word of the Lord hath come unto
me and I have spoken unto you.

Jeremiah 24:3

W·W· NORTON & COMPANY · INC · New York

TO

D. F. R.

Quorum pars magna fuisti

This book includes material originally
published in 1936 under the title
The Prophets of Israel.

W. W. Norton & Company, Inc. also publishes *The Norton
Anthology of English Literature*, edited by M. H. Abrams et al;
The Norton Anthology of Poetry, edited by Arthur M. Eastman
et al; *World Masterpieces*, edited by Maynard Mack et al; *The
Norton Reader*, edited by Arthur M. Eastman et al; *The Norton
Facsimile of the First Folio of Shakespeare*, prepared by Charlton
Hinman; *The Norton Anthology of Modern Poetry*, edited by
Richard Ellmann and Robert O'Clair; and the *Norton Critical
Editions.*

ISBN 0 393 00169 5

PRINTED IN THE UNITED STATES OF AMERICA

567890

Contents

CONTENTS

Foreword

✦ ✦

TO WRITE a book about Greek or Latin literature does not call for any special apologia
from the writer. No one would do so who could not
read Greek or Latin, and interpreters are needed
nowadays when so few can read either. But a book
about the Old Testament written without any
knowledge of Hebrew would certainly seem to
call for an explanation.

Fundamental to my making so unscholarly a
venture was my conviction that for the English-
speaking world the Bible is the Bible in English.
We do not read our Bible as a translation with the
original always in the background of our mind. To
the vast majority of us it is the very Bible itself;
the English words even have a kind of sanctity.
To write about it is not like writing about any
other translation, as indeed it is itself not like any

other. The King James version is the most magnificent translation in literature, and there is no cause for surprise that it has been given the foremost place which in general properly belongs only to an original. For both reasons, therefore, its unique position of supremacy and the beauty and elevation of its style, it seems to me legitimate to write a book based upon it, with no reference to the Hebrew.

How accurate a translation this is can be seen from even a slight comparison with other versions. I have before me the latest Jewish translation of the Old Testament. The Twenty-third Psalm as it stands there begins:

The Lord is my shepherd; I shall not want.
He maketh me to lie down in green pastures;
He leadeth me beside the still waters.
He restoreth my soul;
He guideth me in straight paths for His name's sake.
Yea, though I walk through the valley of the shadow
    of death,
I will fear no evil,
For Thou art with me.

The Jewish translators have wisely kept the incomparable diction and style of their predecessors, and they have rarely found it necessary to alter the meaning. Anyone familiar with the King James version feels completely at home in the Jewish version. In general, I quote from these two versions, in nearly every case using the arrangement of the latter, which distinguishes the poetical parts from the prose. Still, I have occasionally made use of other versions when, as in the book of Job, the accepted translation is now conceded to be incorrect. Several translations of a verse or phrase given in Professor Sachar's admirable *History of the Jews* I have used with his consent.

Throughout the book any date given is to be understood as before Christ.

E. H.

Verily, thou art a God that hidest thyself, O God of Israel.

Isaiah 45:15

CHAPTER I

Many Men of
Many Minds

❖ ❖ ❖ ❖ ❖ ❖ ❖ ❖ ❖ ❖ ❖ ❖ ❖ ❖ ❖ ❖ ❖ ❖ ❖ ❖

THE OLD Testament is not an easy book to read; often it is exceedingly difficult. Many men of many minds wrote it and not only wrote it but rewrote it. For hundreds of years it was edited and re-edited and added to. There was no idea in those days or for hundreds of years to come that a piece of writing must be left just as the original author had composed it. The author was usually anonymous; he did not matter at all. An editor or a scribe was free to insert something of his own. Indeed, it was his duty to improve a piece of writing if he could, to introduce a moral or point one more sharply. The idea that the Old Testament was the unalterable Word of God came very late in its history—A.D., not B.C.—probably a few years after Christ's death. The process of its growth with pious men perpetually trying to make it more edifying is a curious contrast to its later state when it became inviolably fixed, each letter holy and never to be altered. But until then emendations were in order.

One result of this freedom to make additions was that conflicting statements crept in, to the reader's distress. It is baffling and irritating as well to come upon a verse which is a flat contradiction to what another verse has just said. But once it is understood how the book came to be what it is the disagreements cease to give trouble. The Old Testament is not the creation of men who all thought alike because God told them what to think, but of men who had different points of view and sometimes diametrically different. A contradiction may mean no more than that an editor whose piety was greater than his sense for logic tried to insert some orthodoxy into an unconventional piece of writing.

Job and Ecclesiastes are perhaps the best examples of this kind of working over to make an independent thinker fit into the accepted scheme. Both books had originally a clearly developed theme. That is far from the case now. It is often hard to discover any coherent train of thought in them. Again and again the argument is brought up short by a statement which makes nonsense of it. Ecclesiastes as it was first written developed implacably the thesis, Life has no goal and no meaning. It begins with that statement, more eloquently phrased than in any writing before or since: "Vanity of vanities, saith the Preacher, vanity of vanities; all is vanity. What profit hath a man of all his labour which he taketh under the sun?" It is a great pity therefore, the Preacher thinks, to regard life seriously, and the ambition to understand it is just a device of God's to worry mankind: "And I gave my heart to seek and search out by wisdom concerning all things that are done under heaven: this sore travail hath God given to the sons of men to be exercised therewith." Keep sane then, and do not think it better to be wise than foolish: "For in much wisdom is much grief: and he that increaseth knowledge increaseth sorrow."

Death is the end of all; still, there may be just a question mark: "Who knoweth whether the spirit of man goeth upward, and the spirit of the beast goeth downward to the earth?" But the suggestion is not really considered. "All are of the dust and all turn to dust again. . . . The living know that they shall die, but the dead know not anything. . . . Their love, and their hatred, and their envy, is now perished."

No warrant, accordingly, is conceivable for the faith that God acts always for the best; experience shows precisely the reverse, since "There is one event to the righteous and to the wicked; as is the good, so is the sinner." Nevertheless, it is possible if one stops trying to understand why things are as they are to get a good deal of enjoyment out of life by making the most of every pleasure, "eating bread with joy and drinking wine with a merry heart and living joyfully with the woman of thy love."

This completely amoral document was emended by one troubled copyist after another, each so enthralled by the author's wit and wisdom that he could not condemn the whole work, but determined that it should carry good moral lessons, too, for future readers. Inevitably, of course, the thread of the discourse is continually being lost. Pious sentiments are scattered thick, regardless of how little they fit in. Just after "And I saw the wicked buried and they entered into their rest, but they that had done right were forgotten," come the reassuring and incongruous words, "It shall be well with them that fear God. . . . But it shall not be well with the wicked . . . because he feareth not before God." A little farther on a corrective is provided for the dismaying assertion, "There is a just man that perisheth in his righteousness, and there is a wicked man that prolongeth his life in his wickedness." Someone added, "For he that feareth God shall come forth of them all."

These emenders sometimes went very far. There was a strong possibility that the moral additions might not be given weight in view of the undeniable attractions of the original writer, his cynicism lit up with wit and humor, his irresistible love of life along with a keen insight into its evils. It was even possible that with all the additions duly noted and weighed people might perceive that it remained a most pointed and disturbing attack on the justice of God. To guard against both dangers an end was attached to it, completely illogical, but containing an apology for the author and an antidote for the reader. The author, the chapter states, was no doubt wise, "he taught the people knowledge . . . and sought to find out acceptable words." All the same, books are of very little account and a correct point of view is of first importance: "My son, be admonished: of making many books there is no end and much study is a weariness of the flesh. Let us hear the conclusion of the whole matter: Fear God and keep his commandments: for this is the whole duty of man." Those words are still kept as the conclusion of the book which begins, "Vanity of vanities; all is vanity."

Even more drastic changes were made in Job,

and with greater reason. Job charges God directly with evildoing. He himself has done right throughout his life. There is no justification, no excuse even, for the terrible afflictions God has sent him. But against God a man is helpless.

> If it is a test of strength, he is surely superior.
> But if it is justice, who can call him to account?
> For he is not a man as I am,
> That I should answer him. . . .
> Let him take his rod away from me,
> And let not his fear terrify me:
> Then would I speak and not fear him. . . .
> Oh that I knew where I might find him. . . .
> I would order my cause before him.
> And fill my mouth with arguments. . . .
> But I cannot behold him.
> He hideth himself that I cannot see him.

God is judge as well as accuser. Who, however righteous, can maintain his cause against Him? Nor is there a future life where the balance can be redressed. "Before I go whence I shall not return, even to the land of darkness and the shadow of death; a land of darkness as darkness itself; and of the shadow of death . . . where the light is as darkness."

The problem the book propounds is the same as in Ecclesiastes: How can justice be ascribed to God? The spirit, however, in which it is put forward is the very reverse of the good-humored, make-the-best-of-it attitude which stamps that genial essay in cynicism. Job finds nothing good anywhere. In God is only irresponsible power. There is wonderful writing in the book; much of it is poetry of a high order. Even more than Ecclesiastes the Hebrews could not reject it. They did their best to make it over. They attached it to an old tradition of a patient and submissive man who was grievously afflicted of God because God had boasted about his virtue to Satan and Satan had declared that it was due only to his prosperity. Take that away, Satan said, "and he will curse thee to thy face." The rest of the story was about Job's exemplary behavior under all possible misfortunes —above all, how he spoke the beautiful words, "The Lord gave and the Lord hath taken away; blessed be the name of the Lord."

To this primitive and pious tale the main part of the book was tacked on. It is as amoral as Ecclesiastes, but the tone is profoundly, terribly serious. It is black pessimism unrelieved. The subject is a struggle, held to be hopeless from the start, to reconcile the facts of experience, what actually takes place in the world, with faith in a righteous God. It ends, as it begins, with Why? There is no answer; there can be none. Man is born to trouble as the sparks fly upward and clean hands and a pure heart are no defense.

This powerful and despairing presentation of

the basic problem of human life was not only given a conventional moral preface, but two different endings were added to it, first some splendid nature poetry which praises God as almighty and unsearchable and suggests that Job's attitude to Him should be unquestioning submission, and then a happy conclusion which shows that everything that had taken place was for the best. God, after giving Satan a free hand, took over Himself, and Himself refuted Job's charges against Him by heaping upon him greater blessings than those He had taken from him. He gave Job fourteen thousand sheep and six thousand camels and a thousand yoke of oxen and a thousand she-asses, two thousand more in all than those he had lost. And for his dead children, seven sons and three daughters, God gave him an exact numerical equivalent; he had seven more sons and three more daughters. "So the Lord blessed the latter end of Job more than his beginning." It is clear that the poet of the great nature poem was never responsible for this part of the story. A very naïve and prosaic soul produced that proof of God's justice.

Job's charges against God were left essentially unrefuted. His arguments that there was no justice in heaven were so much stronger than anything his comforters urged on the other side that the only possible course to keep the book for the religious was to insert contradictions. Directly after a pas-

sionate declaration on Job's part of his innocence
and the wrongs God has done him: "The Almighty
hath vexed my soul. . . . But my righteousness
I hold fast and will not let it go: my heart shall
not reproach me as long as I live," some editor
put into his mouth a long account of how God
afflicts only the wicked: "This is the portion of
a wicked man with God. . . . If his children be
multiplied, it is for the sword: and his offspring
shall not be satisfied," and so on, with misfortune
piled upon misfortune up to the end when men
"shall hiss him out of his place."

In the midst of Job's still fiercer accusation that
God has "delivered me to the ungodly, and turned
me over into the hands of the wicked" . . . "not
for any injustice in mine hands," but of His own
irresponsible will, some dismayed defender of
orthodoxy made him say, "Behold, my witness is
in heaven and my record is on high. My friends
scorn me: but mine eye poureth out tears unto
God." And after the even worse indictment of
God, when Job says sternly, "Let him slay me.
I have no hope, but mine integrity I will maintain
in his very face," someone tried to nullify the words
by adding, "He also shall be my salvation: for an
hypocrite shall not come before him." The most
familiar passage in the book, the one oftenest
quoted, is the work of a pious emender and a very
good writer. Originally the text read: "Why do ye

persecute me as a stag, and are not satisfied with my flesh? Ye should say, Why persecute we him, seeing the root of the matter is found in me." These two sentences, clearly consecutive, are now separated by five verses in which are the well-known and beautiful words beginning, "I know that my redeemer liveth." That emendation saved the book more than all the rest put together. It proved that Job in spite of his bitter resentment was really a good and God-fearing man.

It is most probable that all direct contradictions are to be explained in the same way. Undoubtedly this is true in the case of the Prophets. Many a stumbling block was presented to the orthodox by those unconventional teachers who thought purely and entirely for themselves. They could not be disregarded. They had to be fitted into the accepted scheme, no matter what violence was done to their argument in the process. For example, in the writings of the great poet who wrote much of the last part of the book of Isaiah, the view that God is a Hebrew deity has been dropped. He is the God of all: the ends of the earth shall sing His praise; the Persian is His anointed; the nations that know Him not shall come to Him; light has arisen for the Gentiles; strangers shall be joyful in His house of prayer. And then, after chapters informed with this spirit, one comes upon the verse: "O Jerusalem, the holy city: for hence-

forth there shall no more come into thee the uncircumcised"—the only time the rite of circumcision is mentioned in the book, much less declared
to be essential to the worship of God. Indeed, with
the exception of Ezekiel, for reasons which will
be explained, this is the only verse in all the
Prophets which speaks of circumcision as demanded by God. The prophets were not at all
interested in ritual. Some pious and patriotic Hebrew added that verse with the best intentions.

It is curious that these champions of orthodoxy
never, apparently, altered or omitted statements
objectionable to them. They seem to have felt
free only to add corrections. Among the widely
different ideas of God the Hebrews were at lib-
erty to pick and choose which they preferred. It
is truly remarkable that although the Old Testament writers were preoccupied with God, although everything turned upon Him, they did not
care to give any consistent account of Him. Lofty
vision, primitive notion, they left side by side.
They never made a theology about Him; they
never put Him into a creed, unless the simple
assertion, the categorical imperative to all Hebrews, may be so considered: "Hear, O Israel,
the Lord our God the Lord is one." Except for
their monotheism, an orthodoxy of belief was
never in their minds; orthodoxy was required only
in the realm of conduct. The Ten Commandments

were binding upon everyone, but irreconcilable statements in the matter of supreme importance did not trouble them. This fact, the knowledge that contradictions in the Old Testament are, so to speak, in order and mean no more than different points of view, removes one great cause of difficulty in reading the Bible.

Even so, the Prophets remain very hard reading. Partly the reason is that one grows weary of exhortations and denunciations, a method of writing which they prefer to any other and which of all methods is perhaps the least appealing to us today. It is a fact that the rolling invectives, magnificent if taken a little at a time, when continued through page after page, chapter after chapter, cease finally to have any power over the attention; the words lose their meaning. There is no climax anywhere; each condemnation of wickedness and threat of punishment to follow is as tremendous as can be; the effect is as if a peal of thunder kept on, never abating, and in the end the mind feels deafened and dulled. All the Prophets suffer from this kind of monotony. Not one of them makes any attempt to lead his hearer up to a height of indignation. They start us on the height and expect us to stay there.

Furthermore, much of this furious anger and passionate reprobation is directed against evils that no longer have any meaning—"the treachery of Edom," "the pride of Moab," the boastfulness of "Rabbah of the Ammonites," the evil doings of "Gog, the land of Magog, the chief prince of Meshech and Tubal." Such references are on nearly every page. Of course these forgotten places with their strange names were alive then; the issues at stake were vital, and the prophets were not men withdrawn from the world, contemplating eternal verities. They lived with intensity in the life of their times and they were on fire to set it right. All this geography of theirs is natural, really inevitable, but it is hard to make one's way through it.

And, as a culmination, one often comes upon a verse which makes no sense at all, even sometimes two in succession. There is no question here of contradictory statements, but of completely senseless statements. It is bewildering to find them in this Book of books, read and studied as no other book. Why have they been left like that, one wonders. If the scholars could not emend them so that they did mean something, why were they kept in the text? It is not good for us to read nonsense reverently; to do so we must turn off our thinking powers and the odds are that we will keep them turned off for the rest of the reading and, especially in the case of the Prophets, run the risk of missing something of unsurpassed wisdom and beauty. Examples of verses without sense are only too easy to find. In the thirtieth chapter of Isaiah there are two, not connected, but near each other: "And his (the Lord's) breath, as an overflowing stream, shall reach to the midst of the neck, to sift the nations with the sieve of vanity: and there shall be a bridle in the jaws of the people, causing them to err. . . . And in every place where the grounded staff shall pass, which the Lord shall lay before him (the Assyrian), it shall be with tabrets and harps: and in battles of shaking will he fight with it."

These are extreme cases, it is true, and yet they can be duplicated many times over, and the effect of them is distracting to anyone who is trying intently to perceive the permanent value of these great men.

The highest elevation in the thought of the Old Testament is reached in the Prophets and the Psalms. The two together give in every significant detail the account of the relation between the divine and the human. In the Psalms, however, man speaks to God. In the Prophets God speaks to man. It is of the greatest importance that additions made by those who were altogether unworthy to be spokesmen for God should be recognized and disregarded.

Therefore he said that he would destroy them, had not Moses his chosen stood before him in the breach, to turn away his wrath, lest he should destroy them.

Psalms 106:23

The meek will he guide in judgment: and the meek will he teach his way.

Psalms 25:9

CHAPTER II

The
Pentateuch

❖ ❖

THE OLD Testament is the account of a people's progress in the knowledge of God. The
book was not written for that purpose. No single
purpose definitely binds it together. It is on the
face of it a collection of documents selected for
no apparent reason: a history of the Hebrew nation from the creation of the world to about
450 B.C.; a number of religious writings, the Psalms
and the Prophets; an assortment of wise sayings
and one of love songs; and a few pieces that do
not belong under any one head, the stories of
Ruth and Esther, the ironical essay that is Ecclesiastes, and Job, half essay, half poem.

It would seem on the face of it hard to find any
dominating thought in writings so diverse, but it

is evident at once by merely turning over the leaves that whatever the ruling ideas of the book may be, a chief subject in it is God. He is not mentioned in either Esther or the book of love poems, the Song of Solomon, but everywhere else His name is found practically on every page and usually many times on each. The men who wrote the Old Testament, the historians, the poets, the story tellers and the rest, saw everything connected with God. But what He was, what they conceived this God to be Who was of supreme importance to them, is not easy to discover. In fact, it is impossible to make a consistent portrait of Him from what the writers say about Him; their descriptions do not agree; sometimes there are even direct contradictions.

In the Pentateuch, held by the Hebrews to be the most important part of the Old Testament, the idea most frequently emphasized is that He is in an unhuman category, all-powerful and not only able, but determined, to visit with terrible penalties those that disobey Him. There are few descriptions of Him; the longest are in the two songs of Moses, but chiefly He is known by the plague, the earthquake, and the storm, His instruments to chastise wrongdoers. He is occasionally described indirectly. He is called the Fear of Isaac, and Jacob says, "How dreadful is this Place! this is none other but the house of God"; and Moses must "put off thy shoes from off thy feet, for the place whereon thou standest is holy ground."

Side by side with these suggestions of One awful and unapproachable, there are accounts of a humanly acting and a humanly comprehensible God. Early in the book of Genesis He is described as walking in the garden in the cool of the evening, a deity with pleasantly familiar ways and anything but terrifying. A few verses farther on He is moved by entirely human motives when He discovers that Adam and Eve have eaten of the fruit of the tree which was "to be desired to make one wise." When the guilty pair have confessed, "the Lord God said, Behold the man is become as one of us, to know good and evil: and now, lest he put forth his hand, and take also of the tree of life, and eat, and live forever; therefore the Lord God sent him forth from the garden of Eden, to till the ground from whence he was taken." Of course God is all-powerful here, but He is easily understood, the way Zeus is in Homer, a person, not a fearful embodiment of wrath, ill defined and awfully remote.

He appears in an equally reassuring light when He tells Abraham that rumors have reached Him about the wickedness of Sodom and Gomorrah and that He is going to investigate and find out if they are true. "I will go down and see whether they have done altogether according to the cry of it which is come unto me; and if not I will know." This is a comfortable statement of God's ways. He acts sensibly and also fairly. Before taking any irrevocable steps He will see for Himself how things are. He is companionable, too. At a feast He shares in the pleasure of food. When an animal is sacrificed the Lord enjoys it as well as the people. They eat part of it and He "smelled the sweet savour" of the part burned to Him on the altar.

It is difficult to make this quite human personage one with the God of terror, but they are often brought close together in the Pentateuch. They are seen almost side by side in the nineteenth and twenty-fourth chapters of Exodus. In the first passage God descends to Mount Sinai in "thunders and lightnings and a thick cloud upon the mount, and the voice of the trumpet exceeding loud," and He proclaims that only Moses and Aaron shall go up to Him: "Let not the priests and the people break through to come up unto the Lord, lest he break forth upon them. . . . And all the people saw the thunderings and the lightnings and the noise of the trumpet and the mountain smoking: and when the people saw it, they removed, and stood afar off. And they said unto Moses, Speak thou with us and we will hear: but let not God speak with us, lest we die." Then, soon after and apparently in the same episode, the Lord bids not only Moses and Aaron to "come up unto the Lord," but also "Nadab" and "Abihu" and "seventy of the elders of Israel." This they do with no fear at all "lest they die," and "they saw the God of Israel: and there was under his feet as it were a paved work of a sapphire stone. . . . They saw God, and did eat and drink," of heavenly food, it would seem, dispensed from the sapphire pavement. Different people wrote those chapters with a very different idea of what God was, and throughout the earliest parts of the Bible He appears in both guises, the aloof and awful God Who declares, "There shall no man see my face and live," and the approachable God Who comes to men in familiar ways, and Who "spake unto Moses face to face as a man speaketh unto his friend."

Morally both Gods are on an equally low level. To be sure, before the Bible begins, the worst of the old fear-worship with its terrible requirements had passed away. The glimpses given of God throughout what are said to be the oldest parts show Him far removed from the savage and lust-ful deities who required of their worshipers "every abomination which the Lord hateth; for even their sons and their daughters they have burnt in the fire to their gods." Human sacrifice had become abhorrent to the Hebrew chroniclers by the time the earliest Biblical stories received their final shape. Even the idea of it is found only in two, Abraham and Isaac and Jephthah's daughter. A wicked king would now and again revert to it, and it is reasonable to suppose that it lingered long among the people to be used in times of danger; indeed, Jeremiah and Ezekiel both refer to an outbreak of it in their day; but there is nothing except sternest condemnation of it in the literature. The God of the Hebrews when we first see Him does not demand to be propitiated in horrible ways. He has become in some sort the Father of His people. He is a father, however, terrible in His severity and implacable if offended, capable of savage and bloody reprisals.

There is no ethical standard for Him. When Abraham passes Sarah off for his sister the man who takes her innocently on this supposition is "plagued by the Lord with great plagues," until he sends her back; Abraham goes quite unscathed. It is God Who hardens Pharaoh's heart not to let the Israelites go, and the motive ascribed to Him is: "I will harden the hearts of the Egyptians; and I will get me honour upon Pharaoh and upon all his host."

It is a long time before the most ordinary morality is ascribed to Him. In the second book of Samuel God bids David to number the people, but when the census is taken, even though He commanded it, He is angry and sends a pestilence which destroys seventy thousand people. The injustice of this procedure is apparent to David, and he asks God why they who had nothing to do with the census should suffer. "What have they done?" And he prays as a man of honor, "Let thine hand be against me, and against my father's house." This story was too much for a later writer. In Chronicles, written hundreds of years after Samuel, it is retold, but Satan, not God, moves David to take the census.

The first book of Kings is given widely different dates by widely different scholars, but it was certainly written or, perhaps, rewritten long after Samuel, and the lively little tale in the twenty-second chapter shows that truth was as yet far from God. "I saw the Lord sitting on his throne, and all the host of Heaven standing by him at His right hand and His left. And the Lord said, "Who shall persuade Ahab, that he may go up and fall at Ramoth-gilead? And one said on this manner and another said on that manner. And there came forth a spirit, and stood before the Lord, and said, I will persuade him. And the Lord said unto him, Wherewith? And he said, I will go forth and I will be a lying spirit in the mouth of all his prophets. And he said, Thou shalt persuade him and prevail: go forth and do so. Now therefore, behold the Lord hath put a lying spirit in the mouth of all these thy prophets."

This irresponsible God would be good to His people if they gave Him perfect submission, but any disobedience enraged Him. The God of Moses was always in a state of perpetual wrath, and He remained like that for a long time. "And the anger of the Lord was hot against the children of Israel and he sold them into the hands of their enemies. Whithersoever they went the hand of the Lord was against them for evil." He admitted no excuse for ignorance. "If a soul sin through ignorance in the holy things of the Lord, he shall make amends for the harm he hath done." The best intentions made no difference. When the ark was being moved on a cart and seemed about to fall, so that the man with it put his hand upon it to steady it, "the anger of the Lord was kindled against Uzzah and God smote him and there he died by the ark of God." Perfect innocence even did not move Him to spare. He not only caused the earth to swallow up the men who rebelled against Moses' leadership, but He made "their wives and their sons and their little children" to go "down alive into the pit." When Moses sang the praises of the Most High he represented Him as saying, "I kill and I make alive, I wound and I heal; neither can any deliver out of my hand. I will make mine arrows drunk with blood and my sword shall devour flesh, with the blood of the slain and of the captives."

This appalling deity had but one claim upon his worshipers. Power was His, limitless, to be exalted and adored. As David is represented praising Him:

> Then the earth shook and trembled,
> The foundations of heaven were moved
> because he was wroth.
> There went up smoke out of his nostrils,
> And fire out of his mouth devoured.
> He bowed the heavens also,
> And darkness was under his feet.
> The foundations of the world were laid bare,
> By the rebuke of the Lord.

There lay the reason why He was to be venerated, and it continued for centuries to be the reason. One of the later Psalms still sees God's praise in

> Fire and hail, snow and vapour,
> Stormy wind fulfilling his word—

This is the exaltation caused by the idea of the glory of sheer power which is so strange to those who are indifferent to the idea of force as such.

God's worshipers were, generally speaking, on a higher level morally than God, but, with a single exception, that level was far from high. The early stories of the Old Testament give a sordid account of human nature. When Abraham, going down to Egypt, is afraid he may be killed by some Egyptian who wants Sarah, for "the woman was very fair," he bids her tell everyone she is his sister. According to the record he does this twice. Isaac when he travels acts in the same way toward Rebekah. Neither man has an idea of running any risk to himself for the sake of his wife. Jacob's mean trick when he stole Esau's blessing is one of a number of mean things he did, and Joseph is like him when he imprisons Simeon and when he has the cup put into Benjamin's sack. Sarah is cruel, driving out a woman and her little son to die in the wilderness. Rebekah cheats her blind old husband. Rachel steals from her father. The women in Genesis match the men.

Considering how natural it is—and how easy —to be romantic about the past and to glorify the ancestors, it is remarkable that with only one exception there is nothing in this first book of the Bible to weight the balance on the other side. All the stories are on the same dreary level; there is not one that glows with high spirit or generosity or nobility. Genesis was written by men who thought human nature a poor thing. The sole exception is Abraham when he prays to God to spare Sodom. It is a noble prayer and a noteworthy exception. Abraham's concern is completely disinterested; he is moved by pure compassion. He is horrified at God's intention to rain down "brimstone and fire" upon the city and all the inhabitants, and he pleads, "That be far from thee to do after this manner, to slay the righteous with the wicked. . . . That be far from thee. Shall not the judge of all the earth do right?" and slowly he beats down God's resistance until he induces Him to promise that He will spare the city if only ten righteous men are found in it. But the story stands alone. There is nothing to be compared with it in respect of elevation until in Exodus Moses comes forward.

Any reader can see without benefit of scholarship that more than one man had a share in Genesis. Besides the two Gods, so obviously the product of different minds, there are two quite distinct accounts of the way the world was created. The first chapter and the first three verses of the second chapter are a hymn of the creation which reaches sublimity, a paean of praise to the Creator, Who in the beginning created the heaven and the earth; Whose Spirit moved upon the face of the waters when the earth was without form and void, and darkness was upon the face of the deep; Who said, Let there be light: and there was light. The other account takes up the rest of the second chapter. It is immeasurably below the first. There is no poetry in it; it is pedestrian throughout. In the first chapter "God created man in his own image, in the image of God created he him; male and female created he them." In the second, "The

Lord God formed man of the dust of the ground, and breathed into his nostrils the breath of life. . . . And the Lord God caused a deep sleep to fall upon Adam, and he slept: And he took one of his ribs, and closed up the flesh instead thereof: and the rib, which the Lord God had taken from man, made he a woman." Man made in the image of God, a great conception greatly phrased, gives way to a tale told in all accurate and impossible detail as if to children.

In Exodus, where Moses is the chief figure, the incompatibilities are even more apparent. The glorious and impossible tabernacle is a case in point. It is supposedly built by wanderers in a wilderness who yet had all the resources of civilization to their hand. The description of it fills eleven chapters and the minuteness of the particulars given is wonderful: "And thou shalt make [God is directing Moses how to furnish the holy place] a veil of blue and purple and scarlet and fine twined linen of cunning work: with cherubims shall it be made: and thou shalt hang it upon four pillars of shittim wood overlaid with gold: the hooks shall be of gold upon four sockets of silver."

The men who placed this costly and elaborate creation in the desolation of the desert so often pictured in the Pentateuch were clearly dreamers, building in their minds a marvelous structure worthy of God. There is another temple of dreams in the Bible, Ezekiel's, when the Hebrews were exiles in Babylon and had no place to worship God. That intolerable deprivation so worked upon Ezekiel, or, some scholars say, a nameless man, that he described in almost unbelievable detail a temple fit for God's presence. So he found his consolation, and so it is reasonable to suppose his fellow exiles found theirs, in thinking out to the last minutiae of measurement and ornamentation a tabernacle of splendor where God could be suitably invoked. They put it all into Exodus. It would be strange if that had been their only addition. Indeed, both Amos in the eighth century and Jeremiah in the sixth give us to understand that they know nothing about the elaborate directions for sacrificing animals which fill so many pages of the Pentateuch. Jeremiah is emphatic: "Thus saith the Lord of Hosts. . . . I spake not unto your fathers nor commanded them in the day that I brought them out of the land of Egypt, concerning burnt offerings or sacrifices: but this thing commanded I them, saying, Obey my voice and I will be your God, and ye shall be my people." Exiled priests, perhaps, wretched at being deprived of their great prerogative of administering "the law of the burnt offering," wrote out lovingly all the regulations and descriptions and added them to the sacred books.

But it is improbable in the extreme that we

owe to any exiles or later writers the portrait of
Moses. The account given of him is wonderfully
vivid and completely consistent. Whenever he appears the pages of the Pentateuch come to life,
except, of course, when the wonderful dreams in
Babylon are put into his mouth. In this connection it is noteworthy that even in Genesis the
various editors and emenders seem not to have
touched the descriptions of the patriarchs. The
picture of Jacob, of his marked peculiarities, could
not be the result of patchwork. The outline is too
sharply given; nothing is blurred or contradictory.
Abraham's prayer about Sodom is not a contradiction. The first of the patriarchs is always shown
as being of a mild temper which might in all
reason be shocked into a protest by God's pro-
posed course of action. But most of them all Moses
stands out as a completely consistent person down
to the last particulars. He is a man of marked
individuality, notably unlike any other Biblical
character. It is clear too that he was great enough
to stamp his personality upon his own age so
powerfully that later and inferior additions would
not be tolerated.

He led his people into the wilderness out of
the civilized world to which they belonged, with
a determination that never wavered, and yet in
the record he has no self-confidence, no desire
whatsoever to be a leader, indeed, a great re-

luctance to put himself forward. His distinguishing characteristics were humility—meekness, the chronicler calls it—and its close companion, disinterestedness, qualities so foreign to the conception of leadership from his day down to ours, it is incredible that they could have got into his biography for any reason except that they were pre-eminently his. When God puts it upon him to go to Pharaoh and demand that he let the Israelites go, he feels helplessly inadequate and is terrified. He tells God, "O my Lord, I am not eloquent, neither heretofore, nor since thou has spoken unto thy servant: but I am slow of speech and of a slow tongue," and gladly when God permits him he gives his brother the prominent place and himself stays in the background. The two go to the Israelites and then "Aaron spake all the words which God had spoken unto Moses and did the signs in the sight of the people." The same thing happens in the interviews with Pharaoh, at least in the earliest version. Aaron is the one who makes the demands on the king and brings the plagues upon the Egyptians. All eyes are turned to him as he does magical deeds at court before Pharaoh and "the wise men and the sorcerers," and stretches out his rod and turns "the waters of the land" into blood. Moses is hardly seen; he is there as his attendant merely—the greatness that cares nothing for the appearance of greatness.

The whole task of leadership was his, the whole responsibility; there was not one person he could share it with; the showy Aaron was a feeble soul. The story of his resolution and tenacity and his devotion to the poor-spirited people he had to deal with is familiar to everyone. Once when he found them worshiping the golden calf he showed the passion of anger he could feel. He dashed down and broke "the tables" of awful holiness "written with the finger of God." His people had chosen an idol in the place of God; they had tried him too far. Everywhere else he takes his stand with them before God no matter what evil they have done or how they have turned against him. He seeks God's favor for them, never for himself. "Pardon our iniquity and our sin," he prays after the idol worship.

Two little incidents recorded of him are striking illustrations of his selflessness, his pure disinterestedness. When a loyal adherent runs to tell him that other men are taking it upon themselves to prophesy and so are usurping his great prerogative of being spokesman for God, and the young Joshua starts up and cries, "My lord Moses, forbid them," Moses' answer is enough by itself to set him on a height few reach. "And Moses said unto him, Enviest thou for my sake? Would God that all the Lord's people were prophets and that the Lord would put his spirit upon them." He wanted no special mark of God's favor. He wanted nothing for himself.

This appears even more beautifully after the worship of the golden calf, when "Moses returned unto the Lord and said, Oh, this people have sinned a great sin, and have made them gods of gold. Yet now, if thou wilt forgive their sin—and if not, blot me, I pray thee, out of thy book."

These words show the kind of man he was, as, indeed, all his words do, except, of course, when he was represented as a high priest of ritual and an architect. Into his mouth was put the endless series of minute rules and regulations which fill many long chapters in the Pentateuch, never ascribed to Moses himself, but to God, Who dictated them to him. Apart from these all that he said bears his own stamp. He was never the typical heroic leader. To standardize him or fit him into the conventional frame would have necessitated making him over altogether, and his historians would not do that—more probably, could not. Therefore he lives for us, a unique as well as a very great man. If the Ten Commandments go back to him it is not a matter for surprise. He was extraordinary enough to have conceived that what God chiefly wanted from His worshipers was morality, justice and chastity and integrity.

The record of his death is singularly fitting and singularly characteristic of the man who wanted nothing for himself, who would not have cared for so much as a stone to mark his burial place. Even he, the records say, the friend of God, even he sinned as every human being does. The story of his sin is told several times and the accounts do not agree, but somehow he displeased God. How not? a Hebrew would ask. "The heart is deceitful above all things, and desperately wicked: who can know it?" Moses too must share in the common burden of humanity, also in its suffering, equally inevitable in the eyes of those who wrote the Old Testament. No transgression without punishment. Moses could behold the promised land in its beauty, but he could not enter it. He could not cross Jordan. The Hebrews with their instinct for grandeur could tell briefly and simply and adequately the story of what happened. He died alone with God as he had lived alone with Him. "So Moses the servant of the Lord died there in the land of Moab, according to the word of the Lord. And he buried him in a valley in the land of Moab . . . but no man knoweth of his sepulchre unto this day."

With his death the Pentateuch ends.

Then the Lord will make thy plagues wonderful.

Also every sickness, and every plague, which is not written in the book of this law, them will the Lord bring upon thee, until thou be destroyed.

And thy life shall hang in doubt before thee: and thou shalt fear day and night, and shalt have none assurance of thy life.

In the morning thou shalt say, Would God it were even! and at even thou shalt say, Would God it were morning! for the fear of thine heart wherewith thou shalt fear.

Deuteronomy 28:59, 61, 66, 67

And it shall come to pass, if ye diligently hearken unto me, saith the Lord, to bring in no burden through the gates of this city on the sabbath day, but hallow the sabbath day, to do no work therein; then shall there enter in by the gates of this city kings and princes . . . from the mountains, and from the south, bringing burnt offerings, and sacrifices, and meat offerings, and incense, and bringing sacrifices of praise, unto the house of the Lord.

Jeremiah 17:24, 25, 26

CHAPTER III

Fear and Form
in Religion

❖ ❖

WORSHIP is a most curious matter. It is not surprising that it should be so, for it is an expression of the strangest thing within us, the religious impulse, the usual, almost invariable, expression. It has its roots in the dim ages of unrecorded antiquity. As far back as the anthropologists and the archaeologists can take us, we find mankind convinced that the visible and the tangible are not the whole of life. There are spiritual forces that mold human fate, stronger by far than all there is in the world men see and handle. Ancient man believed that with as complete a conviction as we do. But to him these forces were wholly outside of himself; he had never an idea that there was anything within him which could alter the face of the earth for the good or the evil of those living on it. All that the human spirit could do in those early days of the world was to people the air with invisible beings, generally hostile, but yet appeasable by human effort.

Worship was born of fear, said the great Roman poet, Lucretius; but human things are never as simple as that. Other ideas and motives had their part; nevertheless as time went on fear took precedence of them all. Primitive man, we can believe, was swayed by the zest of life as well as by the fear of pain and death, but man as he appears in the first written records when civilization was well on its way worshiped chiefly because he was afraid, and the reasons for both his fear and his worship are easy to see. Even today the universe is not a comfortable habitation for the human spirit. Pascal's "The eternal silence of those infinite spaces terrifies me" expresses our common feeling on a clear night of stars; and for all her triumphs, science has not penetrated or made less poignant to our hearts the mystery which touches every one of us most nearly, the question no one can escape from asking, why we are here.

If all our knowledge still does not avail to lighten our darkness, the case of those who lived in ages past was dark indeed. Men long ago were so ignorant, so at the mercy of circumstances. Storms, earthquakes, pestilences, had no assignable cause;

there was no defense against them. They were awful, incalculable manifestations of a dread and hidden power, of whom a man must go in terror all his days. And apart from calamities on a great scale everyday life was a desperate struggle, with disaster always close at hand. Why did evil happenings come and why did they go? Human nature is so made that it must try to understand as well as to overcome. The demons or the spirits or the gods were the result of men's effort to explain. Since they were an explanation found by frightened people, creations of terror, they were generally malignant as well as mysterious. Early Babylonian records have much to say about them. Almost any one taken at random shows how terrifying they were. A description of a spirit who controlled disease is typical. He, the record runs,

Flames like lightning, tearing above and below,
Like a whirlwind besetting a man,
Killing that man.
Driving through another like one whose heart has been
    torn out,
Assaulting his life, in league with death,
Like a great storm whose course none can follow,
Whose goal no one knows.

Here the malignancy is stressed; in the inscription that follows, the mystery has perhaps the chief place, but both are always present in the fear:

Seven are they, seven.
In the deep they are seven.
Neither male nor female are they.
Wife they have not, child they produce not.
Mercy and pity they know not.
Prayer and petition they hear not.
Seven are they, they are seven.

Those two selections could be duplicated over and over again in the writings that have come down to us from that ancient Mesopotamian world, far advanced though it was from the ways of primitive life. In civilized Babylon men lived with that kind of terror pressing upon them. Some way out had to be found.

Human nature will not give up in helpless despair even when the contestants are as unequal as a mortal man and a host of immortal spirits. Early mankind stood up valiantly in that contest. He devised ways in which these forces for evil could in some sort be modified by human action. Of course, they were not easy ways. A God of terror can be won over only by terrible means. Those men of long ago were realists; they did not look to get something for nothing. Great divine favors must be purchased at an equivalent price. In one country and another stories have come down of dreadful deeds done under the all-compelling power of the worship that sprang from fear. One of them is the Old Testament story of Abraham and Isaac, when "God did prove Abraham and said, Take now Thy son, thine only son Isaac, whom thou lovest, and offer him for a burnt offering. And Abraham bound Isaac his son and laid him on the altar upon the wood and took the knife to slay his son. And the angel of the Lord called to him out of heaven and said, Lay not thine hand upon the lad, for now I know that thou fearest God, seeing thou hast not withheld thy son, thine only son, from me." The tenderness of the story with its re-iteration of "son," "only son whom thou lovest," as well as the happy ending, shows how far the narrator was separated from the times when such things were possible, but how ineradicable the memory of them was. So Athens, too, the city of high endeavor in all ways of civilization, kept re-cords of such dark deeds carried out, when no merciful deity had intervened to spare. These are found in the story of more than one favorite heroine of tragedy, notably, the young Iphigenia, who was killed, Aeschylus said,

> When the ships could not sail,
> And the food
> Failed throughout the Grecian camp.
> And all her prayers,
> Cries of Father! Father!
> Her maiden life,
> These they held as nothing—

Every other claim they held as nothing in comparison with what their worship demanded. By pain and loss and agony and death they proved what their belief meant to them. There was little lip-service in the religion of fear.

To look upon such worship as senseless and devoid of any meaning because it was false, is altogether to misjudge it. Of course it was a monstrous superstition without a shred of truth to support it, but it was very far from being senseless; it had meaning, vital meaning. It was real in those days of long ago. Nothing can be important without being real. All that we feel important is just as real to us as all that we live by practically. The worship that centered in fear was of the very first importance, as men proved by the way they acted, the one and only way the reality and the importance of anything can be proved. Whatever is important and real to us affects our actions. Whatever we leave completely out of account when we are deciding how to act, is shown beyond all question to have no reality and importance for us. The old inscription on the gate of Aberdeen University reads, "They say— What do they say? Let them say." The proud words express some people's reaction to public opinion. It has no real meaning for them; they do not consider it in making a decision; their lives are not influenced by it. But to others it is a foremost reality, a factor of paramount importance, affecting everything they do. A man puts himself in one class or the other solely by the way he acts, the one and the infallible test of what is important to him.

When something held to be important proves not to work out in practice, it loses its reality:

> "I can call spirits from the vasty deep."
> "—Why, so can I, or so can any man;
> But will they come when you do call for them?"

If they never come they will not stay real. That is what has happened to the elves and fays once so important in English farmhouses, where "faery Mab the junkets eat" and the lubber fiend in one night "threshed the corn, which ten day-laborers could not end." People discovered that they did not do these things; they did not do anything, and they were dismissed into the realm of the unreal along with all that has been proved by the slow experiments in the long laboratory of human life to have no value for life.

To turn the pages of history is to see how few realities are immortally real, and how many, many transient realities have had a decisive influence upon mankind. How compelling and universally real hell once was and today to how limited a degree, so that it is on its way to becoming altogether unreal. The old terror it sprang from has ceased to work and hell has ceased to matter to us. What blood has been shed and what suffering endured for that, to us, shadowy figment, the divine right of kings. And yet it would be wrong to conclude that the unreal is the same as the untrue. Reality has actually very little to do with truth; there is no necessary connection between the two. Truth may be as unreal as fiction. The real world, the world we live in, is a place of form and color, of "seas and sunsets, trees and flowers, men and women, kings and popes and members of parliament." The true world is a strange, remote, scientific matter of "protons" and "neutrons," a world with which we can make no connection except through our minds, to which we can do nothing, which has no effect upon our lives. It is truth never to be touched or seen, forever unreal. Nothing could be less real to us than the fourth dimension; it will never attain to reality unless some future scientist discovers how people can live in it. The ether-waves were a long-demonstrated scientific truth and completely unreal until Marconi made them real. On the other hand, Jeanne d'Arc's voices were real enough to win battles and set a king upon his throne.

The measure of the reality of a belief is not the actual truth there is in it which can be proved scientifically or mathematically or economically or logically or any other way, but only what those who hold it do about it, how far they act upon it, how much they will sacrifice for it. That is why the blood of the martyrs has been the seed of the church. Those who die for what they believe give the final proof of its reality to them. Looked at from this point of view, early worship has claims upon our respect. It was not meaningless to Abraham or to Iphigenia's father; it was not superficial or formal or sentimental. It was real, terrifically real. Like the martyrs, ancient men proved that what they believed was more important to them than anything else.

In that early worship as we see it in the records left by the oldest outposts of civilization, along with the sacrifice there grew up the ritual of the sacrifice. It was not enough to offer the god something precious; it was necessary to offer it in a certain way. People would make a sacrifice for rain; if the rain came, they would try the next time to reproduce every detail of what they had done before, to repeat in the same order every word they had said. They would remember that they had stood to the left of the altar; then they must do so again; and then to stand to the left of the altar became as important as what was being sacrificed upon it. The most worthy offering could be made worthless, even dangerous, if the right order of words was not followed, or if a man stood in the wrong place or bowed in the wrong way.

This point of view spread as people grew more civilized. In great walled cities life was easier and terror less pressing. Bloodthirstiness diminished in the gods as well as in their worshipers. Indeed, the gods often ended by being tolerably amiable beings whose favor, once purchasable only at the cost of pain and death, could be obtained at no greater expense than carrying out correctly a ceremony—plus, of course, the money-payment always exacted by priests. But paying a tax is not a reality as compared with offering up a son or daughter. The demands of worship were centered more and more in what went on in the temple, and affected less and less the daily life outside. The ritual took the chief place. It became the object of attention, not what was put on the altar. The matter of importance was not how precious the actual offering was, but how accurately the sacrificial rite was performed.

Codes of complicated performances grew up, by following which a man could feel assured of divine favor. There are a number of them in the Old Testament: "And the Lord spake unto Moses saying, Speak unto the children of Israel that they bring thee a red heifer without spot, upon which never came yoke. And one shall slay her and the priest shall take of her blood with his finger and sprinkle before the tabernacle seven times. And one shall burn the heifer and the priest shall take cedar wood and hyssop and scarlet and cast it into the midst of the burning. And a man that is clean shall gather up the ashes of the heifer and it shall be kept for a water of sprinkling: it is a purification for sin."

The immense reassurance of such injunctions lay in the fact that they were at once so practicable and so minutely detailed. They could be carried out with absolute accuracy and they required a painstaking care which resulted in a sense of achievement. This feeling was greatly heightened by the conviction that any failure to carry out the rule might have fearful consequences: "And the Lord said unto Moses, Take unto thee sweet spices, stacte and onycha and galbanum with pure frank-incense: of each shall there be a like weight. And thou shalt make it a perfume, a confection after the art of the apothecary, tempered together, pure and holy, and thou shalt beat some of it very small and put of it in the tabernacle where I will meet thee; it shall be unto thee most holy. . . . And the sons of Aaron took either of them his censer and put fire therein and put incense thereon and offered strange fire before the Lord which he commanded them not. And there went out fire from the Lord and devoured them and they died before the Lord."

This "death before the Lord" shows how a ritual tended to become fixed. In time any growth, even in greater elaborateness, would be checked by the fear of change, always strongest where worship was concerned because no reasoning from cause to effect was possible there. The gods had been observed to favor a worshiper who bowed once or stamped his foot twice, but there was no telling why they did and therefore no telling if they would like more bowings or stampings. A stage would be reached when no deviation at all was permitted. To substitute, even with the most pious intentions, anything that was designed as an improvement, would be regarded as abominable.

Through the ages, too, another strong reinforcement grew up against would-be improvers and reformers: rituals tended to grow beautiful. Their crudeness was modified; artists developed them. The elevated feeling called forth by beauty worked to substitute for a cowardly fear a sense of awe, which is fear purified from personal terror, a sense of the transcendency and the unsearchableness of the deity; and the emotion aroused by beauty added to that aroused by awe forms a combination powerful to resist change. When Solomon dedicated "the house of the Lord, it came to pass when the priests were come out of the holy place, also the Levites, the singers, being arrayed in white linen, having cymbals and psalteries and harps and with them an hundred and twenty priests sounding with trumpets; as the trumpeters and singers were as one to make one sound in praising the Lord, when they lifted up their voice with the trumpets and cymbals and instruments of musick and praised the Lord saying: For he is good, for his mercy endureth forever . . . then the glory of the Lord had filled the house of God." Such beautiful forms of worship would perpetuate themselves. When the emotional appeal they made had developed to the point of being able to bring to pass within the awe-struck worshiper the conviction that the very deity was present with him, they were practically sacrosanct from change.

Ritual grew fixed; it could not any more be used to express this or that immediate need. Life means change, and ritual ceased to keep step with life. Men's view of the world did not remain the same but the forms of their worship did.

When the reason people performed this or that rite was to appease angry spirits thronging around them, their ritual was grounded in life and full of immediate significance. Upon the due performance of it might depend safety, happiness, everything good. It was no stately ceremonial, endeared by long tradition, beautifully elevated above life's squalor. It was a vital effort for self-preservation —this very day, this very hour. There was no idea of worship for the sake of worship. It was a most practical necessity, the ancient equivalent of a gas-mask, with an active enemy perpetually launching a gas offensive. But as the gas-mask proved on the whole effective—people did continue to live and some even to prosper in spite of those dreadful powers—men grew used to the mask and then positively attached to it. The gas offensive became by degrees less dreaded, not only because men felt that they had in the ritual a protection, but also because civilization civilized the spirits as well as their worshipers. But the gas-mask had become by now a part of the scheme of things; it could not be discarded. People did not ask what meaning it had for life, they loved it for itself; they would not be seen without it. It was no longer a means, it was an end.

The old fears passed away. New fears took their place, yet with a difference. The old had had a driving power strong enough to change the very fundamentals of human life; the new were only shadows of that tremendous reality. The gods who loved human sacrifice were gone; the terror which could make men destroy their dearest would never be felt again. But the ceremonial which had come into being because of the terror remained in full force. The form stayed on when the substance which had shaped it had in large part fallen away. The ritual was a vital matter only as long as people were terrified of what they did not understand. While they believed in an omnipotent power which was malignant and incalculable, there could be living reality in the performance of a series of more or less elaborate movements or the repetition of a more or less complicated form of words. The careful carrying out of this rite or that had then a clear meaning for life. It was the indispensable defense to thrust between the god of the lightning or the demon of plague and men's weakness and fear-filled hearts. But when with milder human ways came milder gods there disappeared the idea upon which the whole structure of propitiation had rested, that worship was directly connected with life and that the reason for worshiping was to improve the conditions of life.

The ritual was now seen as something altogether superior to life. It might perfectly well be carried on in a sacred language incomprehensible to the worshipers; it was always accompanied by a code which commanded and forbade many things of no consequence whatever from the point of view of the good or ill of living people. The sacred and profane actions which made a man clean or unclean might have no connection with either moral or physical cleanness. "And the Lord spake unto Moses, saying, Thou shalt not sow thy field with mingled seed: neither shall a garment mingled of linen and woollen come upon thee." This substitution of shadows for realities, of wearing a ritually correct shirt instead of offering up one's child upon the altar, lifted such a crushing load from men, they set no limit to it. Just as the burning of children to Moloch in Carthage shows how far fear could drive a man, so the sacred prostitutes in Babylon show how all-powerful the ritual could be over the fact. Moral cleanness was not only inferior to ceremonial cleanness, it dropped out of sight. The temple prostitute was the woman who was holy, clean, and pure.

Worship and life ceased to be connected. The ritual of worship, often beautiful, solemn, awe-inspiring, fitted to voice the common aspiration of the community, held tremendous potentialities, but the great flood of emotion it called forth was not set to work at anything to make life better; it was directed into channels of futility; it was kept within the temple precinct. People were to find in the ritual itself full satisfaction for the feelings it aroused. It was to be performed for its own sake, men's highest service, their first duty. The chief end of man was to glorify God in a temple.

Sacrifice and offering thou didst not desire; mine ears hast thou opened: burnt offering and sin offering hast thou not required. Then said I, Lo, I come: in the volume of thy book it is written of me, I delight to do thy will, O my God: yea, thy law is within my heart.

Psalms 40:6, 7, 8

CHAPTER IV

Amos: Humanity
versus Form

❖ ❖ ❖ ❖ ❖ ❖ ❖ ❖ ❖ ❖ ❖ ❖ ❖ ❖ ❖ ❖ ❖ ❖ ❖ ❖

IN THE EIGHTH century before Christ, all over
the civilized world form had taken the place
of substance in men's creeds. The splendors of
worship grew more splendid, the multitudes of
priests and devotees perpetually greater; ceremony followed upon ceremony; but the spirit that
had informed the temples and the shrines was
gone. The old terror was dying and all but dead.
Behind the magnificence was emptiness. And then
something happened, one of the most important
events that ever happened, which was to result
in nothing less than a completely new idea of
religion, an altogether different relation of men to
God. In a little country of no consequence whatever to the ruling powers, to the two-thousand-

year-old mother of civilization, Egypt, to the fearful, irresistible war-machine, Nineveh, to the caravans and fleets of Babylon the great, a man arose, one man, all alone, to set himself against the force of the whole world's conviction; and after him another and then another, each always by himself against the nations, in all a mere handful of men, who had a vision of a new heaven and a new earth, a new motive power for mankind and a new road to God, and who proclaimed this strange conception with a passion and a power never surpassed in the three thousand years that stretch out between their day and ours.

There is nothing resembling the Old Testament prophets in all the literature of the world. They were prophets, but in a sense peculiar to themselves: their words still embody men's ideals. They say, What ought to be shall be, and the assertion seems not an expression of an unreal optimism, a dream of happy impossibilities, but a prophecy, a demand which commands our allegiance, an obligation we must struggle to fulfill. But they were not prophets as the term is usually understood. They were no dreamers preoccupied with futurity and aware that as long as they stayed there they could not be refuted. Above all, they were not men claiming magical powers. They shook off magic when the whole world was dark with it. Amos, the first of the prophetic

writers, lived a hundred and fifty years before
Thales, the father of Greek science. The Greeks
then were in a magical world where anything
could be the cause of anything else. But with
Amos magical doings ended for the Old Testament. The prophets lived in a grown-up world.
There are no marvelous happenings in any of their
books, with a single exception now held to be
a late addition, the turning back of the shadow
of the sundial for Hezekiah. Jonah's whale and
Daniel in the lions' den are old tales revived by
writers who lived centuries after Amos and the
others, and who have nothing in common with
them, even though they are usually reckoned
among them.

The prophets of Israel were the product of a
people which developed early a contempt for
charlatans and dealers in magic. Intellectually
they were far above their neighbors or their conquerors, above all the rest of the world, indeed,
for hundreds and hundreds of years. As early as
the eighth century Isaiah spoke with scorn of
"them that have familiar spirits, and wizards that
peep and that mutter"—and that terrorized the
world everywhere else far into the Christian era.
He has the same contempt for "the astrologers,
the stargazers," who are "as stubble to those that
seek them"—and who are still with us. The second
Isaiah in the late sixth or early fifth century in

Mesopotamia, land of many idols, puts into sting-
ing words the folly of fools who believe they can
make a god. A man takes a tree from "among the
trees of the forest. . . . He burneth part thereof
in the fire. . . . He roasteth roast and is satisfied:
yea, he warmeth himself . . . and the residue
thereof he maketh a god. . . . He prayeth unto
it and saith, Deliver me; for thou art my god."
The man who wrote that was a miserable exile
in a splendid city, the mistress of the world, and
he knew himself elevated intellectually far above
his arrogant conquerors and masters.

It speaks volumes for the quality of the Hebrew
mind that with the arrival of the prophets magic
was repudiated. From Amos, the first, to Malachi,
the last, there was a succession of great religious
teachers who never declared that they could perform a miracle, and around whose names no
miraculous stories, with that single regrettable exception, were allowed by their followers to grow
up. This has very rarely been paralleled in the
history of religion. It must be directly traceable
to the influence of the prophets, because before
their appearance marvels play a part in almost all
the Hebrew stories. Elisha, according to the Old
Testament chronology, lived less than fifty years
before Amos, and his life and that of his master,
Elijah, are full of miraculous events: iron floats
on the water; poison becomes harmless; a cruse

of oil remains full no matter how much is poured out of it; and so on. But Amos comes and all that sort of thing ends.

His book is the first in the Bible which can be dated with any accuracy. He lived about the middle of the eighth century. There are of course very much older parts, but we do not know with any certainty when they were written down. It might be thought that the language would be a guide, as it is in all other literatures. Hebrew was the spoken language and must of course have been changing as spoken languages do, but whatever the explanation, the truth is that the Hebrew of what are believed to be the oldest and the latest writings differs little. Perhaps the fact that all the books were constantly being revised and worked over may be one reason for the similarity.

"It was in the days of Uzziah, King of Judah, and in the days of Jeroboam, King of Israel." So begins a little book, no longer, really, than one short chapter, which is placed near the end of the Old Testament, the Book of Amos. The year that is meant was about 760, certainly within a decade of that time. Prosperity had come to the two tiny kingdoms of the Hebrews, and in Israel, the northern one, a great festival was being held at Bethel, a town with a famous altar built by an early king of Israel to create in his own country a center of worship which should put an end to his people's dependence upon Jerusalem, capital of the southern kingdom. There had been peace in the land for a number of years, an astonishing condition in those grim days. Damascus, the Hebrews' perpetual foe, had been weakened by attacks from the fearful power of the north, Assyria, which loomed like a black thundercloud over all the civilized world just then. The King of Damascus was thankful to crouch in safety behind his walls, and for the moment Assyria had other interests than crushing little Palestine. So on that day of high festival in Bethel a great crowd was gathered from all over the land. Festivals and religious ceremonies went hand in hand, and the priests were well to the fore. The sacred golden calf, the treasure of the sanctuary and the object that drew the pilgrims there, was of course in the priests' charge, and of course, too, they knew well how to make the most of their position as the directors and the actors of the spectacle the crowd had come to see. We must imagine a priestly procession, splendid with "gold and blue and purple and scarlet and fine linen," a long line of slow-moving sacrificial animals, holy vessels of "cunning work in silver and gold and brass," deep voices chanting prayers, music of "trumpet, psaltery and harp" —all the ceremonial, solemn and stately, in which priests throughout the ages the world over have expressed themselves. But on that particular day

in the little town, the order was suddenly inter-
rupted. In front of the procession, bringing it to
a halt, a wild-looking figure stepped forth, sun-
scorched and weather-worn, a rough herdsman's
cloak wrapped round him. The chief priest, assured that he had before him one of the foolish
ravers who called themselves prophets and got
food from simple people as being holy, bade him
sternly, "Flee thee away into the land of Judah
and there eat bread and prophesy there. But
prophesy not any more at Bethel; for it is the
king's chapel and the king's court. Then answered
Amos, No prophet I, neither a prophet's son, but
an herdsman and a gatherer of sycamore fruit.
And the Lord took me as I followed the flock and
said unto me, Go, prophesy unto my people Israel.
. . . Now therefore hear thou the word of the
Lord: I hate, I despise your feast days and I take
no pleasure in your solemn assemblies. Though ye
offer me burnt offerings and your meat offerings,
I will not accept them. . . . Take thou away from
me the noise of thy songs; for I will not hear the
melody of thy viols. But let justice well up as
waters and righteousness as a mighty stream."
And at that moment in the priest and the herdsman stood personified the pleasing, outward show
and the difficult inward substance of religion, and
for the first time on record, ritual and righteousness confronted each other.

To Amos the issue was straight. There was no agreement between the two. He had had a revelation. In his lonely life as a herdsman he must have had much time for thought, and it is clear from his writings that he had set his mind to thinking out the relations between the rich and the poor, not yet stamped and impersonalized into the problem of Labor and Capital. He knew the ways of the rich. "They lie upon beds of ivory," he said, "and eat the lambs out of the flock and the calves out of the midst of the stall, that drink wine out of bowls"; they "have planted pleasant vineyards" and built "winter house with summer house and houses of ivory"; their heavy, stupid women— women like cows, he calls them—"say to their masters, Bring and let us drink." He knew the poor, too; he had not to go far afield to learn their ways. He saw them "crushed and oppressed," "swallowed up," by the rich. "Your treading is upon the poor," he said, "and ye take from him exactions of wheat . . . who pant after the dust of the earth upon the head of the poor." And these were the men honored at all places of worship, always given the chief seats at holy festivals. He must often have watched them at Bethel, so scrupulous in every observance of worship, forward with incense and sacrifice, keeping the Sabbath with utmost correctness—"They desire the day of the Lord," he said. Perhaps from his pasture-land he could see them crowding the road on a pilgrimage. He had certainly seen them in the market place of this town or that dealing with a wretched debtor. He describes them twice in the same words as "buying the poor for silver and the needy for a pair of shoes."

As he meditated on these things his revelation came to him. Suddenly he saw forms and ceremonies side by side with human welfare and there stood out plain in his sight the scale of the relative importance of the things men do. "The Lord God," he cried, "revealeth his secret unto his servants." "Come to Bethel," he called to the pilgrims, "and do evil. Bring your sacrifices every morning and every three years your tithes, and offer a sacrifice . . . and call out your liberalities to be heard, for so ye love to do . . . I know your mighty sins: they take a bribe; they turn aside the poor from their right." His eyes were cleared to see the important and the trivial as in the sight of God. The worship of God had no connection with pilgrimages and sacrifices, but only with what men did to each other. Ritual and righteousness had no common ground. God was the God of righteousness and He had nothing to do with ritual. He was worshiped in one way alone, when His justice was made to well up as waters and His righteousness as a mighty stream—His justice, which was the defense of those without power to defend themselves; His righteousness, which was the rescue of the helpless from "robbery and violence in palaces."

What was new in this conception was not the idea of righteousness. That had long been in the world. In the ancient Egyptian and Chaldean records are found here and there expressions of truly disinterested action, of honor and personal integrity and kindness and even high responsibility for others in the obligation to help the unfortunate, but nowhere can a trace be found of the idea that these were more important than or in any sense distinct from what the temple services and the priests demanded. One of the best, morally, of the Babylonian records runs:

> Thou shalt not slander. Speak what is pure.
> Thou shalt not speak evil. Speak with kindness.
> If in anger, do not speak out.
> Approach thy god daily with sacrifice and pure incense.
> Fear of the gods begets favour.
> Offering increases life.

And in Egypt the soul pleads before Osiris: "I have not oppressed the poor. I have not made any to weep. I have not diminished the supplies of temples. I have not defrauded the Nine Gods of the choice parts of victims. I have given bread to the hungry, sacrifices to the gods." So, too, in what is held to be one of the most ancient parts of the

Old Testament, close upon the Ten Commandments follows this other, attributed equally with
the Ten to the authentic voice of God: "If thou
wilt make me an altar of stone, thou shalt not
build it of hewn stone, for if thou lift up thy tool
upon it, thou hast polluted it."

Some real idea of moral obligation had begun
to elevate worship. Men had risen to a point in
their thinking when righteousness, too, was demanded along with the ritualistic demands, but
they had not even approached to where they could
see which was important and which was not.
Everything a man was called upon by his religion
to do lay on the same level, all jumbled together
in one undifferentiated mass. Amos was the first
to make the distinction, and with his realization
of what actually mattered a new stage was reached
in thought, a great step forward taken. The essential was for the first time divided from the
unessential. The vital and the trivial in conduct
were shown side by side in sharp contrast and a
standard of values was set which has persisted
from then to now. Men have never been able altogether to disregard it or forget it. That is the
achievement of Amos, and its importance can
hardly be overestimated.

But a completely new conception is apt to be
seen not by one man alone. It is, as it were, in the

air; several catch sight of it at the same time. Amos was closely followed by three men who equally with him tested worship by the conduct of the worshipers and whose standard of what was and was not important agreed with his: Hosea, Micah, Isaiah. In their writings appear clearly the two highways henceforth to be trodden in the name of religion: worship desirable for its own sake, an end in itself, and worship as a means, good only when it results in practical good, its aim to do away with evil. The issue of righteousness against ritual is presented by all of them with a plain logic of cause and effect and a grandeur of passionate conviction no one else has ever equaled. "I am not come to destroy the prophets," said Christ, "but to fulfill." To Him the case had been stated by them once for all and nothing could be added to its cogency.

The beauty of ritual, the pealing organ, the full voic'd quire, the service high and anthem clear, the pious incense from a censer old, all the ceremonial in great temple or church, beloved by poets and artists and musicians, is utterly reprobated by them. These are delights easily obtained. Not so religion. Nor are they mere futilities. Men use them as substitutes for religion, and as such the Lord hates and despises them. Isaiah puts the whole matter in two words, "Wickedness and worship." They are evil, for they lead to self-

deception: sacrifice and ceremony are the screen
men put between their conscience and their lives.
"Vain oblations," said Isaiah, "incense and Sabbaths and the keeping of feast days are an abomination to God. . . . I am weary to bear them,
saith the Lord. Yea, when ye make many prayers
I will not hear. Put away the evil of your doings.
Relieve the oppressed, judge for the fatherless,
plead for the widow. . . . To what purpose is the
multitude of your sacrifices unto me? saith the
Lord. I am full of burnt offerings . . . and I delight not in the blood of bullocks or of lambs. Wash
you, make you clean. . . . What mean ye that ye
grind the faces of the poor, saith the Lord God
of Hosts." The man of ritual is held up for scornful
denunciation by a nameless prophet, probably the
contemporary of the others: "They seek me daily;
they take delight in approaching to God. They
say: Seest thou not how we have fasted? [God
speaks:] Is it such a fast that I have chosen? A
day for a man to bow down his head as a bulrush
and to spread sackcloth and ashes under him?
Wilt thou call this a fast? Is not this the fast I have
chosen, to undo the heavy burdens and to let the
oppressed go free? To deal thy bread to the hungry
and to bring the poor that are cast out to thy house?
When thou seest the naked that thou cover him?"

"I desired mercy and not sacrifice," so God
speaks, said Hosea. "Israel hath made many altars

to sin. Altars are his own—to sin. I wrote for him the great things of my law, but they were counted as a strange thing. They sacrifice flesh for the sacrifices of mine offerings . . . the Lord accepteth them not . . . Israel hath forgotten his maker and buildeth temples. . . . Sow to yourselves in righteousness, reap in mercy." "I am full of power by the spirit of the Lord," said Micah, "to declare . . . unto Israel his sin. . . . The chiefs give judgment for a bribe. The priests teach for hire, the prophets divine for silver. And on Jehovah they lean, saying, Is not Jehovah in the midst of us? Evil cannot come at us." But "Wherewith shall I come before the Lord? Shall I come before Him with burnt offerings, with calves of a year old? Will the Lord be pleased with thousands of rams or with ten thousands of rivers of oil? Shall I give my first-born for my transgression, the fruit of my body for the sin of my soul? He hath showed thee, O man, what is good, and what doth the Lord require of thee but to do justly and to love mercy and to walk humbly with thy God."

This new vision of what God required brought with it a new vision of what God Himself was, in Whose presence was no place for trivialities. From spectacle and show He was completely aloof, from colorful trappings and sonorous formulas and elaborated intricacies of movement and all the rest that made up the drama of worship, so dear to human performers and spectators. He wanted one thing only, men of good will. To worship God was to do what God commanded, and His commandment was to bring about justice and mercy, just precisely this and nothing else. His worship had no connection whatever with anything done in a temple. It had to do entirely with men's actions toward each other. There was no conceivable form of worship which could bring men into relation with Him. The only way to find Him was to do His will.

"Before the gates of excellence the high gods have placed sweat," said the Greek. The four prophets saw the matter in the same way. In the vision they had had of God there was no place for easy religion. "Woe to them that are at ease in Zion," Amos thundered. Comfortable and profitable religion was shut out. There was no profit in religion and it never offered security. On the contrary, it had to be paid for at a great cost; it was a responsibility awful in its consequences. "You only have I known of all the families of the earth: therefore I will punish you for all your iniquities, saith the Lord." In that sentence Amos summed up his and his fellow-seers' view of religious privilege, the privilege of a great opportunity to carry out a great and arduous task, which a man disregarded or fell short of at his peril.

The one, but tremendous, charge laid upon men

of religion was to realize on earth the justice and the mercy of God. To conceive of this in terms of a facile observance, a trifling expenditure, agreeable in the process and guaranteed to return a hundredfold to the investor, was no less than damnable. "From the prophet to the priest they have dealt falsely," said Jeremiah, a century and a half after Amos. "They have healed the hurt of my people slightly, saying, Peace, peace, when there is no peace. I will surely consume them, saith the Lord, and the things that I have given them shall pass away from them. . . . He judged the cause of the poor and the needy. Was not this to know me? saith the Lord." And the plain, un-equivocal words evoke by force of contrast the endless bitter and often bloody disputes which have tried for nineteen hundred years to settle what the knowledge of the Lord—orthodoxy—consisted in. The cause of the poor and the needy played no part in them. But to Amos and those that followed him, where justice and mercy are, there is the knowledge of God and religion, and where they are not, there is no knowledge of God and no religion. This is the uncomplicated creed of the four first and greatest of the Old Testament prophets.

Centuries after the great four this creed had a revival for a brief three years. Christ's saying, "The Sabbath was made for man and not man for the

Sabbath" would have rejoiced the heart of Hosea and Isaiah. That was the way they had looked at so-called holy things, seeing only whether they helped or hindered human welfare, their eyes fixed always upon the one thing needful, setting men free from the wrongs they do each other. "One thing thou lackest," Christ said to the rich young man—casually, lightly, as it were, just one thing —"Sell whatever thou hast and give to the poor." Had Amos been standing by to hear that advice he would have smiled in grim approbation. "Ye shall know them by their fruits," Christ said. That was the prophets' sole standard too. God's worship must justify itself by practical results.

When life and worship had lost all connection, when nothing that men did to each other was important, but only what they did to their god and their priest, it was Amos, Hosea, Micah, and Isaiah who called men in the name of God away from worship out into the streets, away from a ritual to fairness and kindness. And when their great religion of justice and mercy had been diluted with trivialities and ritual had again taken precedence over life, it was Christ who called them back to the prophets: "Go ye and learn what this meaneth, I will have mercy and not sacrifice"— Hosea's words. "All things whatsoever ye would that men should do unto you, do ye even so to them, for this is the law and the prophets." "If they hear not Moses and the prophets, neither will they be persuaded though one rose from the dead."

To all these men religion was a reality, proved true in the only way truth can be proved, by its results. It was permanently real: it always worked. Justice and mercy were its fruits, realities which are immortal, which forever have meaning for life here and now.

If ye thoroughly amend your ways and your doings; if ye thoroughly execute judgment between a man and his neighbour; if ye oppress not the stranger, the fatherless, and the widow, and shed not innocent blood, then will I cause you to dwell in the land that I gave to your fathers.

Jeremiah 7:5, 6, 7

CHAPTER V

The Hebrews:
The Great Realists

❖ ❖ ❖ ❖ ❖ ❖ ❖ ❖ ❖ ❖ ❖ ❖ ❖ ❖ ❖ ❖ ❖ ❖ ❖ ❖

ON THAT DAY in Bethel no harm came to
Amos. All alone in the great crowd, denouncing what the crowd venerated and delighted
in, he was safe. It is to the point to consider what
would have happened in other lands and other
times, in Spain at an auto da fé or in Naples as the
saintly blood liquefied; or, since the insistence that
religion depends upon the absence of ritual is not
really different from the insistence that it depends
upon its presence, what would have been the fate
of anyone who in a Scotch conventicle, where the
holiness of worship without candles was being
maintained, declared such regulations hateful and
despicable to the Lord. Men who have dared to
block these paths to God's favor have done so

again and again at their peril. But Amos said his say and passed on with no one to lay finger on him.

And yet the priests in Palestine were powerful. They made and unmade kings on occasion. In their hands were the matchless weapons priests have ever used to ensure their authority. They cast the sacred lots when a decision of national importance was to be made; they gave oracles and foretold the future; they alone could offer sacrifices to appease the offended Deity. So armed, priests elsewhere have had no trouble in doing away with their opponents. But in Hebrew history one solitary figure after another stands forth against the background of shrine or temple thronged with ecclesiastics and hurls his anathemas at them for their disregard of righteousness, and always the priests fail to silence him.

The reason goes deep down into the Hebrew mentality. The fundamental convictions of the nation were with those stern denouncers of wrongdoing. Even the priests could not eradicate a point of view which was their birthright as Hebrews. We ourselves like to believe that it will be many a long day before an American or an Englishman will be mobbed for defending free speech. Something within us responds to the idea of freedom however much we may be working against it. Something within the Hebrews responded to the idea of ethical conduct no matter what their own lives were like or how comforting they found the pleasant substitute of priestly service and temple sacrifice. Even in the temple itself the chief place was given, not to a ceremonial sanctity, but to the moral law.

The Holy of Holies was the shrine for the one material object the Hebrews throughout their history venerated, the Ark of God, precious not so much in itself as for what it held. It was a chest and within it was the supremely sacred treasure of the nation. A miracle-working relic? A bit of Moses' robe or Abraham's staff or a bone of Jacob or a splinter of Noah's ark? Or a black stone for the faithful everywhere to turn toward in prayer? Such are the things that other nations have enshrined to bless by touch or sight the believer. The Hebrew shrine held two stone tablets inscribed with the austere commandments of the Law: Thou shalt not kill. Thou shalt not commit adultery. Thou shalt not steal. There was never an idea that the sight or touch of them would heal suffering or sin. They had to be practically followed, acted out with pain and effort in the stress of actual life. That was their only merit to men. In no other way could benefit or blessing be had from them. The Holy of Holies to the Hebrew was the law of right and wrong.

From this soil the prophets sprang. They were

the spokesmen of a nation which thought of religion as bound up with what men did to each other. "The Hebrews," says an old Greek chronicler in astonishment, "rear all their children." There could be no exposure of the new-born in a Hebrew community. What Greeks and Romans practiced at the height of their civilizations and thought no shame, was utterly rejected by a little poor and backward country, rude and uncouth to the point of being uncivilized in the eyes of Alexander's generals and Pompey's legions. Rude they might be, poor they certainly were, but they would not expose their children to die. To the Hebrews, with their instinct to test the importance of everything that touched human life by considering how it worked out in practice, there would have been no meaning in a religion which did not enforce the idea of the value of human life. "Thou shalt not kill." That was the authentic voice of religion, pronouncing what was of first importance for men, a reality that could never cease to be real.

The men of the Ten Commandments were realists; they kept their eyes fixed upon life. Religion must require men to act so as not to injure one another. It must make the conditions of living better. The idea never occurred to them that it could call a man away from the world to forego marriage, comfort, pleasure, in lonely contemplation afar from the ways of common life. Religion's province was precisely common life and the ways of ordinary men. The superiority of the celibate and the solitary was never even conceived of by the men of the Old Testament. Life was a matter of human relations. They wanted above all to understand how to live it, and they set themselves to understand mankind.

The Bible is the great book of human experience. We think of it as the book about God, not man, but even though it has only one hero, the Lord God Almighty, and only one avowed object, to express His inexpressible greatness, it is actually concerned at least as much with mankind. The ways of God and the ways of men were equally interesting to the Hebrew writers and nothing else interested them at all. To the first they gave all their unsurpassed poetic power; to the other what was hardly less remarkable in them, their keenness of observation and penetration of judgment, solidly based upon that realistic view of life we call common sense, which was strong in every one of them.

They were intellectualists, bent upon using their minds and seeing the facts, just as the Greeks were, but their facts were different. What concerned the one was not important to the other. The Greeks cared most for ideas that clarified and explained. They were always trying to think things

out. Is the earth really flat? they asked. Is the
sun in very truth Apollo in his car? And what are
all these notions we talk about so easily—justice,
temperance, friendship? Learning and being able
to explain was a passion with them. This state of
mind was unknown to the Hebrews. They never
looked for explanations or tried to find a cause
for anything. Why should they? The one and only
cause was the Almighty God, Creator of all that
is. They scorned the idea that mere man could
fathom the universe.

Where wast thou when I laid the foundations of the
    earth?
Declare, if thou hast understanding.
Who shut up the sea with doors . . .
And said, Hitherto shalt thou come, but no further:
And here shall thy proud waves be stayed?
Knowest thou it because thou wast then born?
Or because the numbers of thy days is great?
Shall he that contendeth with the Almighty instruct
    him?
He that reproveth God, let him answer it.

At God's good pleasure the sun shone and at
His command it gave way to darkness and the
stars of night. Nature's ways were His ways. When
they considered the heavens they saw them as the
work of His fingers, and they questioned only,
What is man, that thou art mindful of him?

In the greater part of the Old Testament the

division between God and His creation is absolute. Both the sublime and the practical were realities to the Hebrews, but the habit of their mind was to keep them apart. The place of the one was in heaven, of the other upon the earth. The farther God was removed from men, so much the farther were men from God. The more the Hebrews thought of Him, the less they thought of them. The Greeks, that other nation of antiquity in which we are spiritually and intellectually rooted, had also a strong sense of the sublime, but they were able to express it in human terms. The Hebrews turned away with horror from any attempt to do this. "Thou shalt not make unto thee any graven image, or any likeness of anything that is in heaven above"—all transcendent excellency, all that we call divine, was so immeasurably above the human that to conceive of it under any human semblance would be to falsify it completely. They saw mankind as poor creatures and life as a bad business. It is never to be forgotten in what a savage and cruel world they lived. Nature herself was savage in Palestine, and the country lay in the path of great warring empires, surrounded too by bitterly hostile neighbors. Life was in literal truth a desperately hard business, and in such circumstances an optimistic view of human nature does not flourish.

The Hebrews found only in their conception

of God any direct expression of the great spiritual force they were endowed with. They could be exalted by His glory alone, Who covered Himself with light as a garment, Who made the clouds His chariots and walked upon the wings of the wind. He was their escape from the suffering and the sordid meanness of life as they saw it with their keen eyes and felt it with their deep power of feeling.

The Romans, on an altogether lower level of intellect and heart, could find theirs in realms of romance peopled by heroes. The Greeks did not want an escape. The world was beautiful and interesting to them and they rejoiced to live in it. They too had set themselves to understand human nature and they had a profound knowledge of it, but when they wrote of Antigone they showed her wholly noble. They fixed their eyes on that side of her because to them that was what was important in her, not the defects which as a human being she of course had. The good was what counted. But the Hebrews were never able to ignore the defects. They could not see man's grandeur, but only his misery. They felt a deep compassion for human wretchedness, far beyond what the Greeks felt, with the single exception of Euripides, but they could not feel exalted by the tragedy of a great soul suffering; they could not feel fired by a hero's death. They were prevented by their nature from ever finding heroes or great souls.

Their intellectual interest was human beings, looked at as a man looks at his neighbors, individuals more or less faulty, each one like, but also unlike, all the rest. This strong bent to individualize did not belong to the Greeks. They were not concerned to note the peculiarities and minute distinctions that mark off one person from another. Their turn of mind was largely scientific and philosophical and a particular man considered as different from everybody else is not a subject for either way of thinking. The scientists and the philosophers have got to ignore him. But the Hebrews did not care for science or philosophy. To know for the sake of knowing, so entrancing to the Greeks, meant nothing at all to them. They had no disposition whatever, in any direction

> To follow knowledge like a setting star
> Beyond the utmost bound of human thought.

The truth they desired was that which had a direct meaning for their lives. They wanted to know the truth about human nature, and they turned upon the search into it all the force and all the keenness of their minds. They had no wish to make it out good or bad, but only to understand it, and they studied people with a cool dispassionateness no scientist could surpass. The chroniclers who wrote the lives of the nation's great men considered them in exactly the same way as they did people in ordinary life, and when they set down all their failings they had no fear of offending their public who would have looked skeptically if not derisively at any attempt to show a man as wholly good and glorious.

Livy sets us all aglow over Roman heroism. The Hebrew writers with even better stories kindle no fire. Moses, the greatest man of the race, is never presented in a heroic light, from the moment he is first told to "bid Pharaoh to let my people go," and, terrified at the perilous mission, begs off until "the anger of the Lord was kindled against Moses," to the end, when he must die as a punishment for sin without entering the promised land.

David, embarking upon a course of mad adventure, killing Goliath, stealing by night into the tent where his arch enemy lay surrounded by soldiers, and carrying off "his spear and the cruse of water at his bolster" to prove that he had had him at his mercy, risking his life perpetually in hair-breadth 'scapes, a shepherd boy who ended as a king, would have become in any other nation in the world a shining figure of romance, only his deeds of glory remembered. But in the Old Testament he is chiefly human, very imperfectly heroic.

The most contemptible act of his life, the murder of Uriah, hard to surpass in point of contemptibility, is written out in detail with no attempt at extenuation. And the Hebrew father teaching his son would call upon him to mark well the story, and realize that "there is none that is righteous, no not one, save only the Lord God."

This dispassionate accuracy is seen nowhere better than in their treatment of women. The Bible is the only literature in the world up to our own century which looks at women as human beings, no better and no worse than men. The Old Testament writers considered them just as impartially as they did men, free from prejudice and even from condescension. What historian of any other nationality writing of a general's great victory, Barak's over "Sisera with his chariots and his multitude," would set down how he cried out to a woman when she bade him go fight, "If thou wilt go with me, then I will go: but if thou wilt not go with me, then I will not go." And Deborah answered, "I will surely go with thee."

Bad women and faulty women are plainly dealt with, usually presented as "the strange woman which flattereth with her tongue" and "taketh hold of the youth void of understanding," and as the quarrelsome, "A continual dropping on a very rainy day and a contentious woman are alike," but the criticisms are always reasonable and well founded. So too is the praise. After a long acquaintance with the remarkable ladies of the romancers and poets of other lands, it is refreshing to stand on firm ground with the author of the last chapter of Proverbs, whose mother, we are told, had taught him, and who had never an idea that woman was the lesser man or some bright angelic visitant. Neither of these strange creatures had come within the writer's field of observation, but he had observed many women and when he took for his subject The Virtuous Woman he had no need to use the wings of the imagination. "The heart of her husband doth safely trust in her. She will do him good and not evil all the days of her life. She worketh willingly with her hands; she riseth also while it is yet night and giveth meat to her household. She considereth a field and buyeth it. She stretcheth out her hand to the poor. She openeth her mouth with wisdom and in her tongue is the law of kindness." An admirable woman, so useful and dependable, so pleasant and comfortable to live with, and so completely unromantic. Not even a sentence about her looks. "Grace is deceitful and beauty vain, but a woman that feareth the Lord, she shall be praised." One cannot help thinking that no young Hebrew, even though possessed of all the eminent common sense of his nation, could look at his sweetheart quite like that.

And indeed the only book in the Bible which strikes a youthful note, the so-called Song of Solomon, gives a very different account of what is to be praised in a woman:

> Behold, thou art fair, my beloved.
> Behold, thou art fair.
> Thine eyes are doves
> Behind thy veil. . . .
> Thy lips are a scarlet thread,
> And thy mouth is lovely.

There is not a suggestion of the beloved's more useful qualities. These poems are all frank and passionate love songs which breathe the very spirit of youth, but it remains an unanswerable question why they were admitted to the Canon by the sober and learned rabbis who sometime in the first century A.D. established what was and what was not the word of God. To do so they had to turn the lover and his beloved into Jehovah and Israel, as strange a transformation as could be, equaled only by that of the Christians into Christ and the Church. Both ideas do seem a severe indictment of the theologic intelligence. That book of youth strayed into the Bible by some unaccountable vagary.

Except for it and for the prophets, the dispassionate, disillusioned writers of the Old Testament all give an impression of being old. They seem the

retired veterans of life's battle. Once they bore
their share of the fighting, but now they stand
apart, observing and meditating, always keen-
eyed and penetrating, often kindly and tolerant,
but aloof, people who have outlived enthusiasms.
Not the prophets. They are not old. They are men
of passion and fire. But neither are they young;
mature, rather, at the point where life is strongest.
The spirit of youth in the Bible is marked by its
absence.

The only human quality the Old Testament
praises with warmth is wisdom, which in the last
analysis is the art of living, hardly to be attained
except through long experience. The fear of the
Lord was the beginning of it, as of everything
good, but wisdom itself was the culmination, the
reward, of the Hebrews' eternal quest to understand life and mankind. It was by no means knowledge for the sake of knowledge. To depart from
evil was the necessary result of it. The wise man
not only knew, he acted wisely. "Ye shall know
them by their fruits." Wisdom's fruits were pru-
dence, industry, discretion, self-control, a peaceable and equable spirit, all qualities of the utmost
value for living successfully and happily with
others. "The wise in heart shall be called prudent
— He that is slow to wrath is of great understanding— A fool uttereth all his mind, but the wise
keepeth it in till afterwards— I went by the vine-

yard of the man void of understanding and lo, it was all grown over with thorns— A good understanding have all they that do his commandments."

Knowledge must discover an intelligent way of living or it would be worth nothing. If wisdom broke down in practice it was not wisdom. "The ear that heareth the reproof of life, abideth among the wise."

This was the point of view of the men Amos and Isaiah grew up under. When they asked themselves if sacrifice and incense made life better, they were applying to worship the test they had been taught to apply to the affairs of daily life: does practical experience show that the result is good? They were above and beyond the rest not because of the realistic way they saw life, but because they caught sight of a new reality, the most important ever perceived. They were the first to see and to urge on the unconscious movement long under way among their nation to substitute love for fear as the motive power in human life. The God the prophets saw, very dimly to begin with, but always more and more clearly, was a God of good will toward men who did not need to be pacified and propitiated.

The shifting of the center of worship away from fear toward love is the most momentous change that ever took place in men's attitude. Love and fear, the two great forces in life, are emotional opposites, with no common meeting ground. "There is no fear in love, but perfect love casteth out fear." They differ in all respects. Love is not affected by the passage of time; fear continually shifts and changes. One form disappears to be replaced by another, in perpetual succession. Love is a constant; fear tends to decrease. Knowledge acts as a destructive force. "And ye shall know the truth and the truth shall set you free"—free from fears become unreal as the truth is perceived that there is nothing in life corresponding to them.

A figure which has altogether passed for us is that of the terror-stricken mother of Ancient Egypt, who never put her baby to bed without pronouncing a charmed formula against malignant spirits seeking the child's harm, actually present, perhaps, beside the cradle: "Run out, thou who comest in darkness, who enterest by stealth. Comest thou to kiss this child? I will not let thee kiss him. Comest thou to harm him? I will not let thee harm him. Comest thou to take him away? I will not let thee take him away." That fear is ended. It will never walk again. But it does not matter how ancient an expression of love is, it is never outgrown. Verse after verse in the Old Testament says for us more truly than ever we can for ourselves what we know of the tenderness and the anguish of love: "Thy friend which is as thine own soul"; "Intreat me not to leave thee, for whither thou goest I will go; thy people shall be my people, and thy God my God"; "The word of the Lord came unto me saying, Behold I take away the desire of thine eyes. And at even my wife died"; "And the king went up to his chamber and as he went thus he said, O my son Absalom, would God I had died for thee, O Absalom, my son, my son."

Love is not time's fool. But old fears have died and new have sprung up endlessly since the tale of David's grief was told, since Ezekiel's wife died or Ruth followed Naomi to an alien land. Nothing founded upon fear can be permanent. Love offers a durable basis to build upon.

There is not a word in the records of Babylon and Nineveh that foreshadows a change from fear to love in worship, but in Egypt during the twelfth and thirteenth centuries before Christ, there are inscriptions that point to it: "Thou who comest at the cry of the poor"; "Thou sweet well, when the silent cometh, lo, he findeth thee." And most specific of all: "O thou who leadest the suffering to a place of pasture, even as a herdman the herds, I love thee and I have filled my heart with thee." But this new and unformulated idea failed to make a real impress. When it dawned Egypt was nearing the end of her power to seek and find. She was turning back to the past as the source of illumination.

The new conception died in Egypt almost as soon as it was born. It was reborn in Palestine never to die. There men felt deeply, as no men ever have more. The Hebrews were marked by their power of emotion. It is shown through the Old Testament to a degree seldom equaled in all the other literatures of the world. Over and over in its pages human feeling is expressed with a depth of passion never surpassed, as in David's lament for his erring son, or Ruth's entreaty to Naomi. It was inevitable that in a nation so endowed with the power to feel, the two strongest emotions, love and fear, should come into sharp conflict and that there, first, love should show itself the stronger.

A force was irresistibly at work, which no obstacle could block—the peculiar genius of the Hebrew nation for understanding life and the human heart. When a man understands another's misery he must feel pity and feel it too as a fellow sufferer. From the first moment we come upon the Hebrews they have within them the germ of the prophets' religion. Its growth is seen first only on earth; it is slow to reach up to heaven, but in the very earliest part of the Bible a tenderness and compassion from man to man are shown which are essentially at one with Hosea and Isaiah and in startling contrast with God. The people expect from themselves behavior altogether superior to what they expect from the Lord.

Their great men are shown as striving by the force of their own pity to move God to mercy. Abraham did so when he pleaded with Him to spare Sodom and Gomorrah. Moses repeatedly stood between his people and the Almighty's angry threat to "smite and destroy them." When "the Lord told Moses [evidently on His guard against Moses' leanings to humanity], Let me alone that my wrath may wax hot and that I may consume them," Moses chose death with his people rather than favor with God.

Extraordinarily, God was held up only for veneration, never for imitation. Ruthless power must be worshiped in heaven, but pity and kindness must be fostered among men. In the four chapters of Exodus beginning with the twentieth, which are held to be the oldest part of the Bible, there are sayings sweet and tender as any that can be found. Side by side with a verse that describes God as one "who will not pardon your transgressions," is the humanity and generosity of "If thou see the ass of him that hateth thee lying under its burden, thou shalt surely release it. If thou meet thine enemy's ox going astray, thou shalt surely bring it back to him." There is a sensitive delicacy of feeling, too, which builds a bridge straight from those ancient Hebrews to modern days across all the centuries of time: "Thou shalt not oppress a stranger: for ye know the heart of a stranger [so helpless in those days, so forlorn and lost] seeing ye were strangers in the land of Egypt." A high sense of responsibility, too, for the helpless is there, which was the seed of Amos' great gospel for the poor: "Ye shall not afflict any widow or fatherless child." Above all, there is the power which is in fact the source of every one of these qualities, to put oneself in another's place: "If thou take thy neighbor's raiment in pledge, thou shalt deliver it to him when the sun goeth down. For it is his covering: wherein shall he sleep?"

Since the contradiction between what God did and what mankind was required to do was not perceived and all these injunctions were held to emanate from Him, their spirit was bound to work, even if indirectly, against the terrible qualities ascribed to Him, and slowly to invest Him with the compassion and forgiving kindness which were the standards for men.

With the prophets this change became intentional and direct. More and more the humanity of God was emphasized by them. In the end He pitied "like as a father pitieth his children"; He comforted "as one whom his mother comforteth"; He fed his flock like a shepherd; He carried the lambs in His bosom and gently led those that were with young. He could even be more tender than human beings: "Can a woman forget her sucking child, that she should not have compassion on the son of her womb? yea, they may forget, yet will I not forget thee."

So the people who saw better than any other what was real and permanently important in life made the discovery that love, the supremely important, life's eternal reality, was not only for men; it belonged to God as well.

I will mention the loving kindness of the Lord according to all that the Lord hath bestowed upon us. . . . For he said, Surely they are my people. . . . In all their affliction he was afflicted: in his love and in his pity he redeemed them.

Isaiah 63:7, 8, 9

CHAPTER VI

Hosea: The Revolt against Reform by Punishment

❖ ❖

AMOS NEVER saw all that was involved in his conception of a God who wanted only justice and mercy from mankind. His belief in God's mercy never interfered with his worship of God's power. It was one of his younger contemporaries, Hosea, who caught a glimpse of the contradiction. He declared, the first man in the world to declare it, that love and not fear was the force that could draw men away from evil to good. Not power but love was the distinguishing characteristic of Hosea's God. This conception had two tremendous implications and Hosea recognized them. He perceived that a loving God could not exercise omnipotence. Love could not compel. Not only was it impossible that a feeling aroused by compulsion should have anything in common with love, but, even more, such a feeling would be abhorrent to love, which could desire only what was voluntarily given. The methods of love were incompatible with the methods of power; where one worked the other was necessarily excluded. A loving God could do no more than seek to arouse love in return for His own love. And Hosea was able to dispense with omnipotence, a fact which marks him out from all the other great leaders in religion.

The second implication of this idea of the pre-eminence of love was that God was a suffering God. When love meets no return the result is suffering, and the greater the love the greater the suffering. There can be no greater suffering than to love purely and perfectly one who is bent upon evil and self-destruction. That was what God endured at the hands of men. He loved them and they turned from Him to pursue what must end in their ruin. He could not save them for He was love and so He could not compel them. Nor could they ever have been saved by compulsion. Only their own love could save them.

This was a conception as new as that of Amos of the important and the trivial in religion, and it went deeper. It did away with the entire foundation of the worship motivated by fear. It failed, of course, to win a following. Fear continued to

be the motive power used by the God men worshiped, but just as in the case of Amos, Hosea's
words were never allowed to drop altogether from
men's minds. They could not be forgotten. To
change men's basic attitude to life, molded and
fixed through thousands of years, might well need
other thousands, but a vision had dawned of a
passage from terror to love, and here and there,
in one person, in two or three, it met with a response. The long process of changing had been
started.

The man who set forth these ideas 2700 years
ago has left behind him the briefest and most un-
satisfactory record of himself. His little book is
barely seven pages long and much of it—as translated—is quite unintelligible. Verse after verse
makes no sense at all. "Ephraim is oppressed and
broken in judgment because he willingly walked
after the commandment." "For they have made
ready their heart like an oven whiles they lie in
wait: their baker sleepeth all the night; in the
morning it burneth as a flaming fire." "Ephraim
hath hired lovers—yea, though they have hired
among the nations, now will I gather them and
they shall sorrow a little for the burden of the
king of princes." That kind of thing makes dis-
couraging reading.

Still worse, the short account he gives of himself, all that is known of his life, is so confused and

told in such an ambiguous manner that it is often impossible to know whether he is referring to himself or to God and whether he is speaking of his wife or his country. The outline, however, can be made out, and the kind of man he was emerges clearly. It is perfectly apparent that his conception of God was in line with his character; it came to him naturally, as a result of the way his mind worked and also of the way his life led him. The story has to do entirely with his marriage, how he married a woman who was false to him. She had many lovers and he put her away, but he still loved her. She was "beloved of her friend, yet an adulteress," and when her lovers left her and she said, "I will go and return to my husband for then was it better with me than now," he took her back. That is the whole of it. The verses that relate it do not form a continuous narrative, but are scattered through the first three chapters, and all put together make up not even a half page.

Except for these there is not a single personal allusion. But something of what that experience meant to him may be gathered from the fact that throughout his book the words he perpetually uses for wickedness in general are harlotry and whoredom and adultery. None of his three contemporaries do this, but where Amos repeats over and over the word transgressions, and Micah denounces especially lying and deceitfulness, and

Isaiah is hottest against greed and arrogance, Hosea sees his country as one that has "gone a whoring from their God," Israel "has played the harlot," "gone after her lovers and forgot me, saith the Lord." The words recur perpetually as nowhere else in the Bible. Evil had taken that shape in Hosea's mind. "I have seen a horrible thing, the whoredom of Israel."

One more statement too seems to have a personal bearing. Hosea makes God say that he will not mark out unchaste and faithless women for punishment because the men are equally guilty: "I will not punish your daughters when they commit whoredom nor your wives when they commit adultery, for the men themselves consort with lewd women and they sacrifice with harlots." This is an astonishing point of view to be found seven hundred and fifty years before Christ. What would a Greek have thought of it, or a Roman, or a mediaeval knight, or a Victorian squire? What did Hosea's friends and neighbors think of it? "Moses in the law commanded that such should be stoned," the men said who brought to Christ the woman taken in adultery. He looked at the angry crowd and the crouching woman and there came to His mind how Hosea had acted toward another such and what he had said in her defense. He knew Hosea's book well; it is one of the prophetic books He directly quoted from. And He answered in words most beautifully and accurately expressive of Hosea's thought: "He that is without sin among you, let him first cast a stone at her." And yet something may be felt in Hosea's plea which is absent from Christ's sorrowful insight; there is a suggestion of a passionate challenge flung to people who had sat in judgment and condemned his wife and himself. The verse is like a ray of light thrown upon what he had had to endure from those around him.

Something then of how he loved and suffered comes through, halting and obscure and involved though the writing is. And when he speaks of what his own life and his own nature had taught him must be the attitude of God who was perfect goodness toward mankind no matter how "treacherously they dealt with him" and how "vilely they defiled themselves," then his words are beautiful and simple and clear. He looked at God through his agony of love and pity. What ultimate meaning could there be for him in the unapproachable majesty of awful power which so sustained and exalted his three fellow prophets? To Amos, God "turneth the shadow of death into the morning and maketh the day dark with night and poureth the waters of the sea out upon the face of the earth: the Lord is his name"; to Micah, under Him "the mountains shall be molten and the valleys shall be cleft as wax before the fire"; to Isaiah,

"He is glorious in His majesty when he ariseth to shake terribly the earth." But Hosea had seen something greater than the most transcendent power. He saw God looking at mankind as a mother at a little stumbling child learning to walk, or as a man at his tired, hungry ox after the long day's ploughing, or as an anguished father at a wayward son. To Hosea God said:

When Israel was a child, then I loved him.
And I called him out of Egypt to be my son.
The more I called, the farther they went from me.
Yet I taught them to walk, holding them on mine arms.
But they knew not that I healed them [when they fell
    and hurt themselves]
I drew them with a man's cords, with bonds of love,
And I was to them as they who lift up the yoke upon
    the neck,
And gently would I give them to eat.
Yet my people are bent to turn from me,
And though they are called to the most High,
None can lift them.

How am I to let thee go, O Israel?
How am I to give thee up?
My heart is turned upon me.
My compassions are kindled.
For I am God and not man,
I will not come in anger.
I will heal their backsliding.
I will love them freely.
I will be as the dew unto Israel;
From me shall thy fruit come.

(117)

These words reached the high-water mark of the Hebrew conception of God.

The tide rose to a height which is still the world's record, but it was very slow in rising. Even to Amos, a few years older than Hosea, God's power was worshipful. He was to be adored because He was almighty. Omnipotence unqualified belonged to Him. Amos' clear eyes saw all that was involved thereby: the omnipotent must be responsible for evil as well as for good, but he accepted the consequence unflinchingly. "Shall there be evil in a city," he asks, "and the Lord hath not done it?" The correlative of incalculable power, which is fear, he appeals to perpetually as the motive for obeying God. Indeed, God's method for making men good is purely and simply to punish them: "I have withholden the rain from you, yet have ye not returned to me, saith the Lord. I have smitten you with blasting and with mildew—I have sent among you the pestilence—yet have ye not returned to me, saith the Lord." But Amos knew above all what was important and what was not. He held unwaveringly to the conviction that although God could right all wrongs and did not, yet, even so, the wronged were His especial charge. He left a tremendous assertion of a God who cared for the helpless and was thereby shown to be a God of compassion. Before that great conception, the God of Vengeance dwindled to insignificance, even though Amos never perceived what he had done.

Micah, who came shortly after Hosea and some twenty-five years after Amos, was the disciple of them both. He too had had a revelation of the God Hosea saw, one who will "gather in the halt and bring in the outcast," and he describes "the Lord's controversy with his people," in words that might be Hosea's own: "He will plead with Israel, O my people, what have I done unto thee? and wherein have I wearied thee? testify against me. For I brought thee up out of the land of Egypt and redeemed thee out of the house of servants." And Israel's answer to the plea is a magnificent summary of Amos. No burnt offerings will please God, not "thousands of rams" or "ten thousands of rivers of oil," but the Lord has shown what He requires, "to do justly and to love mercy, and to walk humbly with thy God."

And yet with all the radiance of the new light that had dawned upon both men in their degree, Amos and Micah held fast to the glory of power. Even Hosea returns here and there to the idea, so old and so orthodox, of the fearful vengeance that is the Lord's prerogative: "It is my desire that I shall chastise them—all thy fortresses shall be spoiled; the mother shall be dashed in pieces upon her children." This was the God of the religion he had been brought up in. He could rise to a conception that banished it, but he could not stay upon that height. Or perhaps it was that the God of Love was so new Hosea could not always think out how He would act. But this at least is true of him, he had no faith in the saving efficacy of punishment or in its inevitable consequence, the faith in power as meritorious and admirable of itself. Neither Amos nor Micah ever saw the contradiction involved in their conception of a God who was to be obeyed because He could "cause the sun to go down at noon" and "make the mountains molten" beneath Him, and who nevertheless did not want from men the kind of obedience that is given to overwhelming force but "required" of them "to love mercy," to have "justice well up as waters," the free and spontaneous offerings of the heart. Only Hosea realized it. Tyranny, although exalted to sublimity, could be nothing to a God who desired what must be in the nature of the case a voluntary offering, what could not exist in the presence of compulsion. Before such a One invincible power had no meaning. What would it profit Him to be "the King of Glory, the Lord strong and mighty, the Lord mighty in battle"? Love, mercy, pity, have no relation to glorious might. Hosea's greatness is that he rejected the idea of power as divine and the idea of anything else as divine except the perfect goodness of perfect love.

But this shall be the covenant that I will make with the house of Israel; After those days; saith the Lord, I will put my law in their inward parts, and write it in their hearts; and will be their God, and they shall be my people.

Jeremiah 31:33

Where there is no vision, the people perish.

Proverbs 29:18

CHAPTER VII

The First Isaiah:
Statesman and Radical

❖ ❖

ISAIAH WAS an important figure in the politics of his day as neither Amos nor Hosea nor Micah was. He was the first of the three prophet states-men, over a hundred years earlier than Jeremiah and Ezekiel, the two others. Statesmanship could hardly have been more needed by a country than by Jerusalem just then. The danger of complete destruction threatened her during a large part of Isaiah's long life. In his youth the other chief town of the Hebrews, Samaria, the capital of Israel, was in fact annihilated, and in his old age Jerusa-lem escaped the same fate only by a miracle, a veritable, supernatural miracle in Isaiah's eyes. But during the years between, his own ability to see beneath the surface of that troubled world and his extraordinary power as a speaker succeeded more than once in averting complete ruin. Indeed, the final miracle that saved the city was, so to speak, necessary only because his advice had not been followed.

The history of the time so far as the Hebrews are concerned is a confusion of petty wars and city feuds and palace assassinations. Israel and Judah were perpetually at odds, with Damascus now on the side of the one and now on the side of the other and occasionally against both. "The Edomites" come into the picture too, and "the Mehunims" and "the men of Ashdod" and "the men of Gurbaal" and many, many others. Tiny kingdoms forever quarreling, fighting the only excitement available. "It was the time of year when kings go forth to war," one of the Bible chronicles says—the way in those days to describe the coming of spring.

They were hardly wars, border raids, rather; the kings not much more than tribal chieftains or the lords of little cities, but each victor in turn was merciless. "They were made like the dust in the threshing," the Bible says of Israel after a victory of Damascus.

That was the way local politics were run in Palestine. World politics differed only by their grander scale. Egypt, Assyria, Babylon, were all perpetually maneuvering against each other and usually fighting. Babylon just then was the least important of the three, and the countries in Asia Minor, looking for a protector from their neighbors, wavered continually between Egypt and Assyria. Hosea told Israel they were like a silly dove without heart, calling to Egypt, going to Assyria. The end of this double-faced policy was that a few years later "Shalmaneser, king of Assyria, came up throughout all the land" to lay siege to Samaria. Egypt, who had accepted tribute from Israel, did nothing to help, but even so the little town gave the terrible Assyrian army plenty of trouble. For three years she held them off and Shalmaneser died before she fell. But when the end came it meant the end of a nation. "The King of Assyria carried Israel away into Assyria—away out of their own land unto this day," and the ten tribes were lost to history.

That was in the year 722 when Isaiah was a young man in Jerusalem. A few years earlier the king had called in the Assyrians to help him against a coalition of Israel and Damascus and from then on Judaea paid them tribute. It was the only wise policy as can be seen now, but it was not an easy way out. Assyria's idea of tribute was based on what she wanted, not on what a country could pay. Once the king was so hard pressed, he had to cut off the gold from the doors and pillars of the temple to raise the amount required.

and when the palace was reduced to such an extremity, the people must have been driven almost past endurance. Samaria had in fact chosen rather to resist even to the point of death. Isaiah's self-imposed task, to keep his people from throwing off the Assyrian yoke, required all he had of character, vision, intellect. For every reason Assyria was hated, and everywhere. No other conqueror in those cruel days approached her cruelty. Egypt was infinitely to be preferred. To be sure she had allied herself with Samaria and then deserted her, but it took more than that to tarnish her glory. In all the world she was the representative of civilization, the center of learning and art and culture and wisdom, venerable, magnificent. There was magic in her very name. Isaiah, pleading against an alliance with her, cried, "The Egyptians are men and not God, and their horses flesh and not spirit." Such was the hold she had on men's imagination. The Assyrians had only terror to set against it, but it was an awful terror, and with the fall of Samaria it came very near. "It reacheth unto the gate of my people," wrote Micah, "even to Jerusalem." For a time, however, it drew no nearer. A new king, Hezekiah, ascended the throne and kept at first to his father's policy of giving what Assyria asked.

All through these years Isaiah had great influence. He made his first political appearance when he told Hezekiah's father not to fear an alliance of Israel and Damascus because both countries would surely go down under the Assyrians. This was certainly eight or ten years before the siege of Samaria, when Isaiah was perhaps twenty-five or thirty years old. In the bewildering confusions of the day, with Egypt apparently so great and yet betraying her allies, with Assyria evidently so strong and yet involved in terrible difficulties with Babylon, he was able to see clearly. He wanted one thing, safety for Jerusalem, escape from Samaria's terrible fate. He understood all the folly, the madness, of the Hebrews trying to play a part in world politics, and when the trouble with Babylon came to a head and the little Asia Minor nations, full of hope, moved to unite with Egypt against Assyria, he threw himself into the opposition. He would not have Jerusalem join them. No alliances, he told the king, no confederacy: "Associate yourselves and ye shall be broken to pieces." He walked about Jerusalem "loosing the sack cloth from his loins and putting his shoe from his foot," declaring that to such a state would Egypt come and all who relied upon her. "Woe to them that go down to trust in the shadow of Egypt." He could see beyond her splendor to her feebleness. First to last he was opposed to any dealings with her.

"In sitting still and in rest shall your salvation

be," he told Hezekiah. "In quietness and in confidence shall be your strength." Under this guidance the tiny kingdom led on the whole a peaceful life in that uneasy world for the first twenty years after the fall of Samaria. But then for some unknown reason things went wrong: Isaiah was no longer listened to. The pacifists were defeated and Jerusalem threw in her lot with the confederacy against Assyria. It was an act of folly so great as now to seem incomprehensible. A few years before, when Babylon was keeping the Assyrian armies busy, there might have been a chance of success, but by now she had been defeated with the thoroughness peculiar to the Assyrian.

The result was that Assyria decided she had better make all safe in Judaea and the countries round about before coming to a final trial of strength with Egypt. So "Sennacherib, king of Assyria, sent his officers with a great host against Jerusalem" and Hezekiah's ministers came out to talk with them. The Assyrians said, "Thou trustest in the staff of this broken reed, Egypt—so is Pharaoh to all that trust in him. But if thou say, we trust in the Lord our God, am I come up without the Lord against this land? The Lord said unto me, Go up against the land and destroy it." The spokesman had a loud voice and he talked in Hebrew and Hezekiah's emissaries were afraid, for the wall above them was lined with listening people. They said—dull men evidently—"Speak unto thy servants in the Syrian language and not in the Jews' language in the ears of the people on the wall." The Assyrian, of course, called up still more loudly: "Hear ye the words of the great king, the king of Assyria. Make an agreement with me and eat ye every one of his vine and of his fig tree. Beware lest Hezekiah persuade you saying, The Lord will deliver us. Hath any of the gods delivered his land out of my hand? Did they deliver Samaria out of my hand?"

But when the words were reported to Isaiah he said, "Thus saith the Lord God of Israel concerning the king of Assyria, he shall not come into this city, nor shoot an arrow there, nor come before it with shields. By the way that he came, by the same shall he return."

And so it happened. Among the Assyrian inscriptions is one which records this campaign: "I, Sennacherib, went to the land of Syria—and Hezekiah, king of Jerusalem, who had not bowed down at my feet, of his strong cities, his castles, and smaller towns, I besieged, I captured, forty-six. Himself like a bird in a cage I shut up inside Jerusalem." He besieged the city, but he did not capture it. Herodotus in Egypt two hundred years later was told a story of an army of mice having devoured all the leather parts of the Assyrians' armor so that they could not fight.

Isaiah's account is: "The angel of the Lord went forth and smote in the camp of the Assyrians a hundred and fourscore and five thousand— So Sennacherib, king of Assyria, departed." And to Isaiah was given the transcendent joy of seeing, plain before his eyes, what was to him a direct intervention of God to save the city of God, a factual proof of his own faith in God and in the glorious destiny of Jerusalem. All that he had suffered under what, in his agony at seeing where everyone else was blind, he called "the burden of the valley of vision," must have been compensated for in full when the Assyrians began to break camp. What St. Paul calls the eternal things which are not seen became to Isaiah the things seen. He believed that his eyes had beheld the invisible made visible.

Nothing further is known about him. He was sixty years old or so when the Assyrians marched upon Jerusalem, and with their retreat he drops out of the Bible. The great voice that has been thundering against evil and exultantly ringing forth promises of future blessedness stops. No reason appears; there is no rounded end. The discourse breaks off as it were in the middle of a sentence; suddenly Isaiah ceases to be. The chroniclers record that "Hezekiah slept with his fathers," but there is not a word to tell us how Isaiah died.

We read him under terrible disadvantages. Many writers had a part in the book called by his name. The last twenty-six chapters are now believed to have been written in large part by a nameless author, the second Isaiah, so-called, with interpolations by other authors, most of whom lived at least two hundred years later than Isaiah himself, and, some say, as much as three hundred. Even among the earlier chapters there are insertions not by Isaiah. One will be reading about Assyria and suddenly come upon a mention of the conquests of the Medes, who were an obscure little tribe, subject to Nineveh, in the days when Isaiah watched the Assyrian advance. In one passage Assyria is the great ruling power of the world; in another Babylon has that place. Even in the parts that seem clearly Isaiah's own the chronology is confused. In Chapter 10 Samaria has fallen; in Chapter 17 she is threatened with imminent destruction; in Chapter 28 she is a city of "glorious beauty," which has only begun to fade. At best Isaiah would not be easy reading, but the way his book is put together places a great and unnecessary obstacle in the way of understanding him. Most bewildering, for instance, is his assertion often repeated that Jerusalem will never be destroyed and the assertion, still oftener repeated, that she shall be utterly destroyed, her houses empty without a man, her land a desolation. Meta-

phor after metaphor points this conviction: **God
will ruin the wall of His vineyard and give it over
to be trodden down; He will lay siege against His
city and cast her low in the dust; He will break
her people into bits like a potter's vessel.** And at
the same time she is God's cherished possession
which He will protect "as birds hovering" over
their nests. In one chapter the Assyrian is the rod
of God's anger, summoned by Him to punish the
city and trample upon her people "like the mire
of the streets." In another it is God who protects
her from the Assyrians and causes them to fall
by the sword, while Jerusalem is "a quiet habitation," "not one of the stakes thereof shall ever
be removed."

These opposing statements come and go perpetually to the distress of the reader. Sometimes,
it is true, Jerusalem's security is referred to a distant future when a righteous remnant of the people will dwell in her, but oftenest it is clear that
the immediate present is meant. In Chapter 10
God Himself bids His people, "Be not afraid of
the Assyrian"; in Chapter 29, the city is to be
brought down to the dust by the multitude that
fight against her; in Chapter 31, God will not let
the Assyrians harm her. It is not possible to make
out what Isaiah really thought. Did his belief that
the Assyrians would destroy Jerusalem belong to
the days when they swept over Israel, just stop-

ping short of Judaea; and did the exulting confidence that God would protect the city come with
the onrush of patriotic devotion when the enemy
was at her walls and the Hebrews were resolved
to defend her to the end, with the same desperate
determination they were to show in Jeremiah's
day? As the book stands, the two points of view
cannot be made rational by separating them in
time, but no attentive reader of Isaiah can put
up with the conclusion that he was a man of mud-
dled mind who did not see when he was contradicting himself. He was one of the great minds
of the world, and the way his book has been edited
wrongs him.

Amos and Hosea are distinct personalities.
Though they wrote so little and were far from
thinking of giving an account of themselves, the
kind of men they were comes through unmistakably. But it is not so with Isaiah. He is a baffling figure. Statesman and prophet have so few
points of contact, it seems impossible to combine
them. Isaiah in his foreign policy was a man of
cool worldly wisdom with a shrewd insight into
the dominant factors that lay beneath the shifting
surface of his world. He abominated Assyria as
none could more, but he would have Jerusalem
submit unreservedly to her. There should be no
mad crusades to overthrow her hateful power if
he could have his way. But this common-sense

acceptance of the inevitable in foreign affairs was diametrically opposed to what he thought ought to be done at home. In spite of the fact that he wanted with passion to save the city and saw with perfect clarity her precarious position, nevertheless he set himself against the men of wealth and position who must be, from any common-sense point of view, her chief defenders. He turned from them with scorn and loathing to champion the poor and the helpless. Also he fiercely attacked the priests and the established church, always everywhere a bulwark of strength to the state, precisely the influence a statesman would conciliate in a crisis. Far from working for a united front in the city at a time of such danger, he stood forth to demand changes in her social structure which were guaranteed to split her apart. The princes that oppressed the fatherless and the widowed, the priests that ministered to a shallow and heartless worship, he declared must go. Everyone "proud and lofty" should be overthrown, "the mighty man and the man of war, the judge, the counsellor, the eloquent orator." God would bring them all to nothing and set up the rule of the weak. The wise and the prudent should perish; the meek and the poor should rejoice.

These two sides of the man cannot be fitted together. The cautious leader who guided his country for years along the narrow path of safety has nothing in common with the passionate reformer, prepared to go all lengths in righting wrongs. Isaiah remains a contradiction. Outside Jerusalem he was a statesman; inside he was a prophet.

The world of Amos and Hosea did not go beyond Palestine. Isaiah knew the great world. With his mind much occupied with foreign affairs, it might be expected that he would give us some clear picture of the ancient civilization we try so painfully to rebuild, but it is not so. Whatever descriptions he has left serve one purpose only: they are fuel for his burning denunciation of the same evil he sees everywhere. Therefore there is no precision of detail, nothing to distinguish one country from another. When all places are equally black, they must all be completely alike. Of course, Jerusalem's sins are more particularized. She is rich and—one may almost say, therefore—full of wickedness. No end to the gold and silver in the great houses, "the treasures," "the pleasant pictures." Banqueting goes on all day; people get up early to feast and drink and listen to music. Bribery is everywhere; judges are bought; the poor have no defense; the priests are drunkards. It seems at first sight odd that none of the tremendous invectives are directed against the evil that is so black in Hosea. Harlots are hardly mentioned. But they have never been considered of any political importance, and Isaiah's care was for the state. The corruption in official life which wealth brings, the greed and the arrogance and the hypocrisy of rich men, fixed his attention.

It may be surprising to discover that the only minutely detailed picture he has drawn is of women's dress; but it should not. Through all the ages the subject has engaged the attention of some of the most serious minds among mankind. Prophet and priest and pope and saint have spent themselves in holding up to execration the clothes women wear. The blame is impartially distributed, now upon sleeves that are too short, now upon sleeves that are too long, knee-length skirts in one generation and those that trail on the ground in the next. It would seem that men always felt the most violent objection to whatever was the fashion. Isaiah's account of the reprehensible attire of his day is extraordinarily detailed, almost like the inventory of a fashionable woman's wardrobe. It is very difficult to imagine him walking about Jerusalem to study each separate bit of the women's finery, but that is what he did. Not a pin or a bracelet escaped his notice. His ladies wear "tinkling ornaments about their feet," and "round tires like the moon" on their heads, and "changeable suits of apparel," and "wimples," and "crisping pins," and "earrings," and "nose-jewels," and so on through all of eight verses, with Isaiah's wrath increasing at each item until in the end he is threatening the creatures who will put on things like that with sackcloth and baldness and "branding instead of beauty."

Apparently none of the invectives, no matter how lofty their source, ever had any effect at all. Prophets and preachers thundered and popes anathematized, but the women went right on wearing what they wanted. A century after Isaiah, Ezekiel, the only other prophet to give the matter a standing among the major crimes, found the daughters of Israel as wickedly clad as ever: "Thus saith the Lord God, Woe to the women who sew pillows to all armholes and make kerchiefs upon the head." The object of these adornments is specifically stated. It is "to hunt souls." "Thus saith the Lord God: Behold, I am against your pillows wherewith ye hunt souls. Your kerchiefs also will I tear and deliver my people out of your hand." There, it may be, lies the reason for this strange frenzy of anger through the ages which seems so out of all proportion to the cause, as well as for the absence of any blame of men's clothes, apparently, from all we know, quite as elaborate and expensive. "Wimples" and "pillows to armholes" and their like have exercised a fatal lure. One cannot escape the conclusion that the fury aroused by them is a tacit confession.

The matter is worth notice here only because of the possibility that it lifts, if ever so little, a corner of the curtain that effectually hides the actual man Isaiah was. One personal experience he does relate and in some detail; it is easy to believe that he looked on it as a turning point in his life. When he was young, perhaps eighteen to twenty years old, standing entranced in the temple he had a vision of God Himself attended by wondrous beings he calls "seraphim," one of whom touched his mouth with a burning coal. The voice of God reached his ears asking, "Whom shall I send?" And Isaiah cried out, "Here am I; send me." The sentence is so young, so full of the generosity which does not count the cost it cannot see. Read in the light of the rest of the book it points to the high spirit which takes instinctively upon itself whatever hard thing is to be done. There for a moment Isaiah himself is seen, but everywhere else he remains a shadowy form that towers up and away from us. But the main line of his thought can be made out even with the vexing contradictions in his book. With him, the point of view of the prophets in general begins to open up.

As compared with the brevity of Amos and Hosea and Micah, Isaiah is long, and in every respect he is a continuation of them. What he says rounds the others out. He did not go off on any new path of his own as Amos and Hosea did, but he went along the ways they had discovered. He was indeed far from seeing the implications of Hosea's idea of love, not power, constituting God's greatness; but Hosea himself had not seen them and no one was to do so for a long time to come. Nevertheless Isaiah recalls Hosea's God in many a verse. He is "the merciful Lord" who is "like clear heat upon herbs and like a cloud of dew in the heat of the harvest," and in whom "the poor of his people shall trust." But at the same time there are long chapters about the fury of His anger and the awful power of His vengeance:

> And the hills did tremble,
> And their carcasses were as refuse in the streets.
> For all this his anger is not turned away;
> But his hand is stretched out still.

It was the same conception the men before him had had. The old God of terror had had mercy and love added to Him, but without any modification of the terror.

Not Amos, but both Hosea and Micah looked forward to a day when God would have punished His people enough and would turn His anger away from them, or at the least, from a repentant remnant. Isaiah caught up this idea and expressed it again and again in words which even when translated are as beautiful as any ever written:

O house of Jacob, come ye and let us walk
In the light of the Lord.

For unto us a child is born,
    Unto us a son is given:
And the government shall be upon his shoulder.
    And his name shall be called
    Wonderful, Counsellor,
The mighty God, the everlasting Father,
    The Prince of Peace.

They shall not hurt nor destroy
In all my holy mountain;
For the earth shall be full of the knowledge of the Lord,
As the waters cover the sea.

It was the goal they all saw. Not to be attained
by men when they are dead, but upon this earth
by the living. Even in the soaring visions of a far
distant future Isaiah kept his eyes fixed upon life.

In general the same outlook and temper of mind
mark all four prophets. Fundamental to the
thought of each of them was the opposition between what is and what men know ought to be.
They saw that life as it is actually lived and the
demands of the conscience are antagonistic. The
discord inherent in human experience was perceived and felt by all of them with incomparable
clarity and intensity, but it was Isaiah who gave
it the greatest expression. It has never had a
greater. Everywhere and in all ages when men
have thought about life they have been brought

face to face with the evil they give rise to and their
own revolt against it, and now and again they
have been able, one here, another there, to put
their knowledge into words so profound or so passionate that they could not be forgotten; but
among them all Isaiah is unsurpassed. He had
the power to see the depth of the division, the
contradiction our life is grounded in—the good
that men would, they do not; the evil which they
would not, that they do—and he had the power
to set it forth:

> Your hands are full of blood.
> Wash you, make you clean.
> Put away the evil of your doings
> From before mine eyes.
>   Cease to do evil;
>   Learn to do well.
> Seek justice, relieve the oppressed,
> Judge the fatherless, plead for the widow.
> Come now, and let us reason together,
>   Saith the Lord;
> Though your sins be as scarlet,
> They shall be white as snow,
> Though they be red like crimson,
> They shall be as wool.

The contrast between the wrong which is and the
right which could be goes through the book in one
splendid image after another:

> For wickedness burneth as the fire.
> Yea, it kindleth in the thickets of the forest

And they roll upward in thick clouds of smoke. . . .
Woe unto them that decree unrighteous decrees.
To turn aside the needy from judgment,
And to take away the right of the poor of my peo-
  ple. . . .
The spirit of the Lord shall rest upon him.
He shall not judge after the sight of his eyes,
Neither reprove after the hearing of his ears:
But with righteousness shall he judge the poor,
And reprove with equity for the meek of the earth.

Isaiah saw as Amos and Hosea had seen—perhaps even more clearly than they—that men did
not want evil even when they did evil. He knew
the force of the appeal that hands red with blood
could be washed clean, that a man might walk
in the light of the Lord instead of the thick clouds
of wickedness. He believed it to be stronger
than any other and absolutely sure to prevail in
the end. Evil would finally be conquered since
men were made by God and so were made for
goodness and were happy only if they were
good.

The people that walked in darkness
  Have seen a great light.
They that dwelt in the land of the shadow of death,
Upon them hath the light shined.

Good and evil he looked at just as Amos and Hosea
had, judging them by the way men acted toward

each other. To do the will of God was to make human life better.

His thought can be put into a very few simple statements: God is, and He is righteous and omnipotent. The purpose of mankind, the reason they are here, is to carry out God's purpose for the world, and this means to right the wrongs men do. Some day they will all be righted and evil will be at an end. This is not a system of thought. There is no attempt in Isaiah to give a coherent account of God and man and the world. He is not a theologian. He is not interested in explanations, not even of the contradictions he is perpetually emphasizing between what men do and what they want, between God's omnipotence and men's power to thwart Him. He gives no definitions and no formulas. All he does is to assert with the utmost majesty and grandeur of which language is capable, that the purpose behind the universe is good and that men can help or hinder its fulfillment. Therefore Isaiah's words still have meaning. Explanations never hold for very long. The more precise and perfect they are, the more quickly they are discarded. We are so made that when we have achieved a system of thought which explains everything beautifully, we have reached the point where we must begin to give it up. We are contented with it only as long as it is incomplete and we are trying to fit things into it. When it is complete we have got to start on something else. Outgrown explanations and abandoned theologies lie all along the path mankind has gone. But the vision of good and the desire for it remain always, and words that throw light upon either are never tossed aside as unproved and untenable. Light needs no proof. It needs only to be seen.

The prophets were men with extraordinary minds, able to reflect greatly upon human life and to see deep into human nature, but they did not care to analyze or explain what they knew. They never looked at it like that. It did not take the form of consciously thought-out ideas to them. Other, lesser men would get ideas from them and take infinite pains to explain them, but the prophets themselves were not teachers; they were discoverers. Something that had been hidden they uncovered, and it was there for everyone to see. No logical commentary could add force to "What mean ye that ye grind the faces of the poor"; no argument is required to prove the truth in "The burden of the valley of vision"; no one needs to defend the injunction, "Judge the fatherless, plead for the widow."

Such words stand of themselves. They are unassailable and they never wear out. Thousands of years leave them the same; time does not touch them. The book of rational knowledge is being perpetually added to and the earlier pages torn out, but Isaiah is not superseded by Christ or Amos by St. Paul. Their truth is true always and the words in which they embodied what they saw of men's dream and their desire, forever stir the desire and make the dream live.

Woe is me! My soul hath long dwelt with him that hateth peace. I am for peace: but when I speak, they are for war.

Psalms 120:6, 7

CHAPTER VIII

Jeremiah:
The First Pacifist

❖ ❖ ❖ ❖ ❖ ❖ ❖ ❖ ❖ ❖ ❖ ❖ ❖ ❖ ❖ ❖ ❖ ❖ ❖ ❖

JEREMIAH was the world's first apostle of pacifism. That singular Egyptian, Akhenaton, who was born some thousands of years too early, appears to have acted like a pacifist, but nothing in the great sun hymns shows him a deliberate advocate of peace. The post was created by Jeremiah, and when he died it was long left vacant.

Pacifism, however, as he initiated it, differed from the kind general today. It was not a protest of the conscience against the evil of war; it was a declaration of the enlightened reason about the folly of war. A hundred years earlier, Samaria, the chief town of Israel, had been destroyed for trying to shake off the yoke of Assyria and Israel had dropped out of history. Jeremiah had that object lesson before him when he began his great campaign to show Jerusalem that it was the part of common sense for the weaker always to submit to the stronger, and that it was better to be slaves than to be dead.

Pacific thoughts of any sort were strange to the world he lived in. The end of the seventh and the beginning of the sixth century B.C. were periods specially marked by violence and terror. Drastic changes on a great scale took place within a few years. The civilized world which preceded Greece and Rome was breaking up. Everywhere was commotion, upheaval. Wild tribes beyond the farthest edge of civilization swept down in the terrible Scythian invasion. Herodotus says they drank the blood of their enemies, using their skulls for cups, and made cloaks out of their scalps. They are often described in the Bible: "Behold a people cometh from the north country. They shall lay hold on bow and spear; they are cruel and have no mercy; their voice roareth like the sea, and they ride upon horses set in array as men for war." When they came they brought the Dies Irae: "A day of wrath, a day of trouble and distress, a day of wasting and desolation, a day of darkness and gloom, a day of clouds and thick darkness, a day of war-horn and battle roar against the fenced cities." Mighty Nineveh shook under their attacks,

so weakened by them that a few years later she
fell before the Babylonians, and the Assyrian Empire, cruelest and most hated of world powers,
came to an end. "Nineveh—pelican and bittern
roost on the capitals; the owl shall hoot in the
windows, the raven on the doorstep." Egypt, for
thousands of years the center of the world, set herself against Babylon's upstart assumptions and
met with a shattering defeat. That was around 600,
a hundred and fifty years after Amos.

All this turmoil seethed around Jerusalem,
never herself greatly given to tranquillity. She had
had to pay tribute to Nineveh, but she refused to
acknowledge Babylon, and Nebuchadnezzar appeared before her walls just as the Assyrian had
in Isaiah's day. But then "the prophet of the Lord"
had bade the people resist and Sennacherib had
gone on his way without reducing the city. This
time God's prophet was the passionate champion
of surrender.

It would seem from the Bible story that the
Babylonians came three separate times against
Jerusalem. One king apparently died in battle;
another was carried off to Babylon "with the
queen and the eunuchs, the princes of Jerusalem
and the carpenters and the smiths." "None remained, save the poorest sort of the people of the
land." But each time when the army had gone
the Hebrews revolted. They were a proud fighting

nation, and also they were trusting to an alliance with Egypt, but Jeremiah told them, as Isaiah had seen a hundred years earlier, that Egypt was fading out of the picture where once she had dwarfed everything: "Pharaoh, king of Egypt, is but a noise; he hath passed the time appointed." When the Babylonians came the third time with the great Nebuchadnezzar himself at their head, they saw to it that this obstinate center of revolt was destroyed before they left.

Throughout these years, certainly well on to forty, Jeremiah never ceased exhorting king, princes, people, to submit to Babylon. The word of the Lord came to him, he tells us, bidding him speak. "Then I said, Ah, Lord God, behold I cannot speak; for I am a child. Then the Lord put forth his hand and touched my mouth and said, Behold I have put my words in thy mouth," and Jeremiah set himself to be God's mouthpiece.

Never in his life afterward did he waver in his conviction that what he thought was the thoughts of God and what he spoke was the words of God. "Thus saith the Lord." The words are repeated over and over again on every page of his writings. All his speeches begin with them, end with them, are punctuated by them. Not he, but the Lord God of hosts demanded the surrender of Jerusalem to Nebuchadnezzar as a punishment for its wickedness.

This solution of the particular form of the problem of evil presented to him was characteristic of the nation. The Hebrews' explanation of why misfortune overtook them was peculiar to them alone and remains unique. No other nation has ever accounted for its sufferings in the same way. They blamed themselves and no one else for what happened to them. Even when Assyria, the detested and detestable, crushed Israel, the Hebrew historians' only comment is, "For so it was, that the children of Israel had sinned against the Lord their God." They do not denounce Assyria at all. Their only concern is the wrongdoing of their own people. "They wrought wicked things to provoke the Lord to anger . . . and sold themselves to do evil in the sight of the Lord . . . until the Lord moved Israel out of his sight."

It must not be supposed that these writers lacked patriotism. The Hebrews' love for their country flames up throughout the Old Testament. Nevertheless, when defeat and exile and the extremity of suffering came upon them, they found the reason in their own wickedness, never in another's.

This extraordinary attitude, never paralleled by any people before or since, is explained by Jeremiah's attitude. What confronted him was the terrible contradiction of an omnipotent God of absolute righteousness and the imminent destruction of the city of God together with the enslavement of God's people. The problem could hardly have appeared under an aspect more acute, but Jeremiah's agony for Jerusalem never made him question the goodness of God. That was the basic fact of the universe. If the ruin of all things was at hand there must be a full and sufficient explanation for it. Justice required not only the defense of the innocent but the punishment of the offender. The suffering he saw around him must be the result of wickedness, the inexorable working out of the justice of God. "Because they have forsaken my law which I set before them: Therefore thus saith the Lord of hosts, the God of Israel; Behold I will feed them, even this people, with wormwood, and give them water of gall to drink." This was a basic Hebrew conviction. God must punish because God was just.

So fortified, Jeremiah was able to persist in the terrible task of opposing the entire nation's fighting spirit aroused to the utmost in a life-and-death struggle. One man against all the rest, and one man urging what seemed to run contrary to everything that was best and noblest, patriotic devotion to fight to the death for one's country, religious devotion to defend to the utmost God's temple. Only base surrender on the other side. High courage, heroic resolution, engaged against dull, flat, not to say ignoble, political expediency and common sense. Never again did pacifism look quite so mean and poor-spirited, and never has there been such a lonely pacifist. "Everyone doth curse me," he said. "I sat alone because of thy hand." It was too much for him sometimes, but never for long. "The word of the Lord was made a reproach to me and a derision daily. Then I said I will not make mention of him. But his word was in mine heart as a burning fire shut up in my bones, and I was weary with forbearing and I could not stay."

They shut him up in prison as the only way to silence him—this was early in his career when the first of the three kings to resist Babylon was reigning—but the only result was that he took to writing instead. He dictated to a scribe "a roll of a book" which said: "The king of Babylon shall certainly come and destroy this land and cause to cease from thence man and beast," and he found means to get it to the king. "Now the king sat in the winter house, a fire on the hearth burning before him," and when he had read "three or four leaves, he cut it with his pen knife and cast it into the fire." It availed him not at all. Jeremiah instantly dictated another roll with "all the words which the king had burned and there were added besides unto them many like words." Why or when they let him go is not told, but we find him next "in the stocks by the house of the Lord," put there by the priest to stop his seditious speeches, quite as futile a method of silencing him as the king's had been. "Then said Jeremiah unto him, Thus saith the Lord, I will give all Judah into the hand of the king of Babylon and he shall carry them away captive."

At first sight it seems extraordinary that they did not kill him. The only explanation he himself gives is that his invariable preface, "Thus saith the Lord," was one no Hebrew could completely disregard. The people said: "This man should not die for he hath spoken to us in the name of the Lord, our God." Something more, however, must have operated to make those who were agonizing and dying for the war keep down their rage when he thundered against it. It was not only that he claimed to speak for God; they felt the flame of God within him. "He was a burning and a shining light," as he spoke to them. Nothing else can explain his strange immunity. But to leave Jeremiah alive was to have to listen to him. He stood in the court of the Lord's house and said to all the people, "Serve the king of Babylon and live, wherefore should this city be laid waste?"

So matters went on during two reigns in Jerusalem and two invasions of the Babylonians. After the king and the nobles and the skilled workmen had all been carried off to Babylon, after such a first-hand experience of the power of the new empire, it is astonishing that the people left behind in Jerusalem were willing to revolt a third time. Their chief men were all killed or in exile; their new king Jeremiah shows up as an utter weakling. They were hardly more than a hillside fortress and the mistress of the world was ranged against them. What desperate devotion to freedom drove them on or what high confidence in the immunity of the City of God, can only be conjectured. They did revolt and for two and a half years of fierce fighting and intense suffering the little city held out heroically against the armies of Babylon.

Through all that time Jeremiah never ceased urging, "Bring your necks under the yoke of the king of Babylon and serve him and live." To the captives in Babylon he wrote advice which was a piece of coolest, calmest reasoning: "Thus saith the Lord, Build ye houses . . . and plant gardens . . . take ye wives . . . and seek the peace of the city whither I have caused you to be carried away captives, and pray unto the Lord for it; for in the peace thereof shall ye have peace." His heart was indeed full of pity for them. "Weep not for the dead neither bemoan him," he said, "but weep sore for him that goeth away, for he shall return no more, nor see his native land." Nevertheless, he saw the matter in the light of expediency and good sense undimmed by emotion; he bade them submit even to the last degree of praying the Lord for the welfare of their masters. It was the only wise policy, exactly like his advice to surrender the city.

And yet as we look at the picture it seems strange to us. The values we are used to are gone. Sensible capitulation instead of dying for a lost cause is rarely held up in the pages of history for our admiration. We are not called upon to honor the peace party in fifth-century Greece and the cities that submitted to Persia's overwhelming force, but the reckless fighters at Marathon, Thermopylae, Salamis. And so it has been throughout the ages. Spartacus in his desperate fight for freedom is presented for our admiration, not the eminently sensible slaves who chose the wiser part of submission to their Roman owners. The little *Revenge* madly engaging the entire Spanish fleet is never forgotten, and the common-sense supporters of the House of Hanover fade beside the irrational and irreconcilable gentlemen who drank to the king over the water.

History, at any rate the history we read in our youth and remember, is incurably romantic. Old Testament history, too, is by no means exempt from the charge. When Gideon sets out to free his country from the Midianites, "and their camels were without number, as the sand by the seaside for multitude," he disdains to meet them with anything approaching an equal force; he sends away his men on one pretext and another until only three hundred are left, and with these "he mightily discomfited the host of the Midianites." No hero can be found anywhere less influenced by the rational. Jeremiah was a new phenomenon and destined to remain the only one of his kind for many centuries.

His political sagacity is not open to question. The cause the defenders of Jerusalem were fighting for was already lost. They could only die and draw down with them the helpless, old, young, women, children, in one great ruin. Of course, surrender meant slavery. Jeremiah never attempted to disguise the fact. "You will be slaves," he told them in effect, "but at any rate you will be alive." To prefer death to slavery was to him folly so great, it positively amounted to wickedness.

It is not that he saw life as more valuable than anything else. In his own life he showed more than once that he was ready to die rather than keep silence when the Lord bade him speak. To do the will of God a man must be willing to die, but only for that. Honor, freedom, pride, patriotism, all such motives were nothing to him when weighed in the scale against keeping alive.

In curious contradiction to the hard common sense that controlled him, he was a man of intense emotionality. He had a warm heart and a great

power to love. He suffered agonies in the suffering
of the people around him. "If I go forth into the
field," he cried, "then behold the slain with the
sword! And if I enter into the city, then behold
them that are sick with famine. . . . Oh that my
head were waters and mine eyes a fountain of tears
that I might weep day and night for the slain of
the daughter of my people." Because of this vehemence and depth of feeling his words burn with
a fire and passion not surpassed anywhere in the
Bible. His indictments of Jerusalem's wickedness
have an awful magnificence.

I beheld the earth,
And lo, it was without form and void,
And the heavens and they had no light.
I beheld the mountains and lo, they trembled,
And all the hills moved to and fro.
I beheld and lo, no man,
And all the birds of the heavens were fled.
I beheld and lo, the fruitful field was a wilderness,
And all the cities thereof were broken down
At the presence of the Lord and before his fierce anger.

. . . .

Run ye to and fro through the streets of Jerusalem,
And see now and know,
And seek in the broad places thereof,
If ye can find a man,
If there be any that doeth justly, that seeketh truth.

. . . .

Pray not even for this people, for I will not hear them,
Can the Ethiopian change his skin,
Or the leopard his spots?
Then may ye also do good,
That are accustomed to do evil.

"I will cause to cease from the streets of Jerusalem the voice of mirth and the voice of gladness, the voice of the bridegroom and the voice of the bride; for the land shall be desolate . . . And death shall be chosen rather than life by the residue that remain."

Nevertheless, with all this emotional intensity his judgments were based upon his reason alone. He saw the heroic defense of the city without a throb of admiration for its reckless courage; recklessness was wicked foolishness. He heard appeals to "Freeman stand, or freeman fa'," with an ear coldly aloof. What did freedom matter to the dead? It was a man's duty to act rationally. It was for Jerusalem in this crisis to follow where expediency and good sense pointed and submit, and for her people, when they became slaves, to be good, docile slaves. So they would soonest better their lot and minimize their sufferings.

To the great and moving appeal of patriotic devotion to die rather than give up being a free nation, he did not oppose another, equally great and moving. He did not say, "Thus saith the Lord,

Thou shalt not kill." He said, "Resistance is folly. It is senseless to throw away your lives." And the people turned a deaf ear to him as in times of difficulty and danger people have always turned a deaf ear to the appeal of the purely rational.

When something of paramount importance is to be decided, the final judge is not the reason reaching a conclusion in cold blood. The mind by itself does not suffice. There are times when its decision must be set aside. Let a useless ne'er-do-weel be drowning and a man of great worth pass by, he must risk his life to try to save him. There is a court which to every one of us supersedes that of reason. When life and death are at stake we act not as our mind would bid us, but at the dictates of one or another of those unassailable if incalculable realities, the emotions. And it cannot be maintained that mankind has only lost thereby. Passion does not always blind; it may reveal a truth not to be discovered in a cool hour. Under stress of emotion men have done what was rationally impossible, and in so acting have raised the standard for human effort. Heroism is never rational and every heroic death sends its imperious challenge down through the generations.

But to Jeremiah as he saw life, any life, that is, except his own, the mind was the one guide to be followed. A man of hot blood governed by cool reason. This paradox of his nature was shown with

ever increasing clearness during the reign of the
last king of Jerusalem. Soon after his accession
the party which looked to Egypt for deliverance
seemed justified. "Pharaoh's army came forth out
of Egypt and when the Chaldeans that besieged
Jerusalem heard, they departed." Then things
went very ill with Jeremiah. His only response to
the lifting of the siege was: "The Chaldeans shall
come again and take this city and burn it with
fire," but he seemed proved a false prophet, and
they imprisoned him "in the dungeon" and starved
him too. He was on the point of death when the
king relented, had him given food and committed
to the court of the prison, apparently a place ac-
cessible to the public, for from it "He spake unto
all the people saying, Thus saith the Lord, He
that remaineth in this city shall die by the sword,
by the famine and the pestilence, but he that goeth
forth to the Chaldeans shall live." Barbed words
to speak just then, for the Chaldeans had returned
to the siege and the people were at the point when
"all the bread in the city was spent." Intolerable
words for those who were putting up a last desperate fight to remain a free nation. "The princes said
to the king, We beseech thee let this man be put
to death for he weakeneth the hands of the men
of war." They let him down with cords into a
dungeon, "and in the dungeon was mire, so Jeremiah sunk into the mire."

It was a eunuch who saved him, one of that strange band who from immemorial times in the East have pulled the wires of palace intrigues. Odd company for Jeremiah, but he was a good friend. He worked on the king's feelings and was allowed to "draw him up with cords." However, the miry dungeon had not had the least effect. Admitted to the king's presence he told him, "If thou go not forth to the king of Babylon's princes, then shall the Chaldeans burn this city and thou shalt not escape out of their hand." But by this time the end was in sight. It may be that when it was too late they began to think that his way would have been better, or perhaps in that terrible hour nothing that any man said could matter. At all events "Jeremiah abode in the court of the prison and he was there when Jerusalem was taken."

It is clear that the Babylonians had heard of him. "The captain of the guard said to him, If it seem good unto thee to come with me to Babylon, come and I will look well unto thee." To accept such an assurance of safety and well-being was most certainly the course dictated by the good sense, reasonableness, expediency, Jeremiah was forever urging upon others. But when it was a question of himself alone he could never be guided by them. In the conduct of his own life they played no part at all. He would have none of that promised ease. Though the city was destroyed and the temple, "our holy and beautiful house where our fathers praised thee is burned with fire," he would stay with the little handful of people left behind to great hardships, even though they had all been bitterly his enemies.

But he had worse than hardship or personal enmity to face. The governor appointed by Babylon was assassinated by a few fanatics, and the whole community was stricken with terror and decided to flee to Egypt. Again Jeremiah was in the opposition, and again he was the whole of it. To him withdrawal to Egypt meant the abandonment of their country in the moment of her greatest need. They would leave her "a desolation without an inhabitant." Any hardship was preferable to that. He told them—the words sound like an effort to rationalize his passionate longing to stay and help revive the beloved land God had given them: "Ye say we will go into Egypt where we shall see no war nor hear the sound of the trumpet [constant in their ears for nearly three years] nor have hunger of bread [the terrible famine of a closely beleaguered city] and there will we dwell. And now hear ye the word of the Lord, O ye remnant of Judah. Go ye not into Egypt. Behold I will send Nebuchadnezzar the king of Babylon, and he shall smite the land of Egypt." But the frightened, broken people would not listen, and they forced him to go with them.

How long he lived in Egypt is not known. Eighteen years after the fall of Jerusalem the Babylonians invaded the country as he had foretold, but he must have died before they came. The last glimpse we are given of him is in keeping with the whole. He is standing before "all the Jews which dwell in the land of Egypt," a furious crowd at the moment, and he is denouncing with stern anger "their wickedness in that they went to burn incense and to serve other gods." The people defied him. They would worship "the queen of heaven," for when they had done so in Jerusalem they "had plenty of victuals and were well." Now they were miserable because they had neglected her. Jeremiah faced them as he had over and over again in the past, and, as always, the angry shouting died away when the people looked at him. Something in his face, in his presence, had power to awe. He said, and they are his last recorded words: "The incense which ye burned in the streets at Jerusalem, did not the Lord remember? Because of the abominations which ye have committed, therefore is your land a desolation, without an inhabitant. Ye and your wives have spoken, we will surely burn incense unto the queen of heaven. Therefore, hear ye the word of the Lord, All the men of Judah that are in Egypt shall be consumed by the sword and by the famine until there be an end of them." So he faced them, an old man, all alone, and so history leaves him. Nothing more has come down about him except a tradition that he was stoned to death in Egypt by his own people.

It was a heroic life, without any of the glamour which is so apt to attend the hero. One man set himself against a nation's patriotic fervor to resist enslavement, and failed to win them over to the cause of safe surrender. That is the whole story. It is not brightened by one ray of the romantic light in which the leader of the lost cause moves. Jeremiah did not lead any cause; he was never able to draw others to his side, and if he had, his cause was not the kind that romance loves. He was able, however, to hold to it unflinchingly year after year with no support at all, able to stand absolutely alone through the long years of bitter siege and desperate defense, able to spend his life with hatred and contempt his only companions. He had enduring heroism, and that must always get on without trumpets or brass bands. It is never scenic; it lacks variety; and it generally ends by boring the spectators. Instead of an enraged people falling on Jeremiah and killing him when Jerusalem was captured—the only appropriate death—they forgot all about him, and he was sitting dully and unimportantly in the prison-court when the Babylonians entered, an anticlimax typical of his whole life. So much so that the tradition of his dramatic end by stoning in Egypt seems more in accordance with the bright-colored records of the early Christian fathers, through whom it has come down, than with the sober narrative of the Old Testament. We may believe without stretching probability that he died lonely and neglected, no doubt, but undramatically in bed—and certainly with his spirit unbroken.

It is often said by Jewish writers that the picture of "the suffering servant" in the fifty-third chapter of Isaiah [written after the return from Babylon] refers to Jeremiah, but the idea cannot stand a moment's scrutiny. It is true that "He is despised and rejected of men" might well be applied to him, as also, "Surely he hath borne our griefs," and "He was bruised for our iniquities"; but when it comes to "He was afflicted, yet he opened not his mouth . . . as a sheep before her shearers is dumb, so he openeth not his mouth," nothing could possibly be less like him. That mouth the Lord had touched was always open, pouring forth grief, appeal, denunciation, and fiercely defending himself too. "Know ye for certain," he cried, "that if ye put me to death, ye shall surely bring innocent blood upon yourselves." Equally unlike him is the end of the great chapter, "and made intercession for the transgressors." That was not in Jeremiah: "Lord, thou knowest all their counsel against me to slay me; forgive not their iniquity, neither blot out their sin from thy sight." Magnificent virtues were his, but there was no place among them for patience and a forgiving temper. He would not have offered harbor to either of them for one moment.

His God, Whom he trusted with an unshakable and never failing trust through the bitter pain and failure of his life, Who was his "strength and fortress and refuge in the day of affliction," Who spoke to him saying, "Be not afraid for I am with thee," was very like him. Great love was one of His qualities. He said, "I have loved thee with an everlasting love; with loving kindness I have drawn thee." A tremendous power of anger was another: "Behold the whirlwind of the Lord goeth forth with fury. . . . The fierce anger of the Lord shall not return until he have performed the intents of his heart . . . and the peaceable habitations are cut down because of the fury of the anger of the Lord." He was a God grandly and majestically conceived: "Am I a God at hand, saith the Lord, and not a God afar off? Can any hide himself in secret places that I shall not see him? saith the Lord. Do I not fill heaven and earth? saith the Lord." Also like Jeremiah, He could be tender and pitiful. He would "gather from the coasts of the earth the blind and the lame, the woman with child and her that travaileth with child. I will cause them to walk by the rivers of waters in a straight way. . . . For I have satiated the weary soul, and I have replenished every sorrowful soul. . . . I will watch over them to build and to plant, saith the Lord." To Jeremiah He was "replenishment" for all weariness and every sorrow. In his great picture of the future, golden streets and gates of pearl had no part; one thing alone sufficed: "They shall all know me, from the least of them unto the greatest of them, saith the Lord." There could be nothing beyond that to Jeremiah.

All for him that escaped the limits of the rational was contained within his conception of God. When he looked at the world he was purely a rationalist. What can the reason do on this earth where brute force is the master? How in that disposition of affairs can goodness and the things of the mind survive? The problem was clear to his piercing intellect; he found but one solution, complete submission. That the way to strength may be through resistance, and that heroism, the mountain peak of resistance, is marked by victory and not defeat, both these ideas he, a heroic resister himself, would vehemently have rejected. The paradox that the hero triumphs because he dies, he never could have perceived, for a paradox is not rational.

O God, why hast thou cast us off for ever?

We see not our signs;

There is no more any prophet;

Neither is there among us any that knoweth how long.

Look for the covenant;

For the dark places of the land are full of the habitations
of violence.

Let the poor and needy praise thy name.

Arise, O God, plead thine own cause.

Psalms 74:1, 9, 20, 21, 22

CHAPTER IX

Ezekiel:
Organized Religion

✦ ✦

E ZEKIEL'S claim to greatness rests on an altogether different basis from that of the other
prophets. His book shows a great falling off men-
tally and morally from them, from Jeremiah whose
contemporary he was, as well as from the earlier
men. He might be passed over quickly as far as
the depth and range of his ideas are concerned,
but the work he did is of first importance. He was
the initiator of the separatist movement which
preserved the Hebrews as a distinct people after
they had lost their freedom. In spiritual elevation
and intellectual power he was far below his predecessors, but in practical efficiency he outdid them
all.

Only one passage in his book recalls the men

who preceded him at their best and highest, his parable of the Good Shepherd.

My sheep did wander through all the mountains . . .
And none did search or seek after them.
Therefore, O ye shepherds, hear the word of the
    Lord . . .
Behold I, even I, will both search my sheep
And seek them out.
As a shepherd seeketh out his flock . . .
So will I seek out my sheep,
And will deliver them out of all places
Where they have been scattered in the cloudy and
    dark day.
I will feed them in a good pasture . . .
I will feed my flock,
And I will cause them to lie down, saith the Lord God.
I will seek that which was lost,
And bring again that which was driven away:
I will bind up that which was broken,
And strengthen that which was sick . . .
And ye are my flock.
The flock of my pasture are men,
And I am your God, saith the Lord God.

This has the true ring of the great prophets. Hosea could have written it or Micah or Isaiah, but it stands by itself in Ezekiel as regards both its style and its substance. It is his only reference to the God of love. His mind was bent with fierce concentration on the God of power. The threats that fill chapter after chapter of what God's implacable anger will bring down on man's wickedness outdo Isaiah and Jeremiah together.

But the fact ought not to tell too much against him. It was the result of his passionate loyalty to the Lord of hosts. In those days gods shared the fate of their worshipers. If a country was defeated so too were her gods. Judah's defeat, complete as none could be more, was in the eyes of the world the conspicuous defeat of God. So Ezekiel must emphasize, almost to the exclusion of everything else, God's eternal, omnipotent power. It is true that God's city lies in ruins, God's people are helpless captives, the heathen have triumphed, religion is trodden under foot. Well, what is proved thereby? Nothing, answers Ezekiel, nothing at all —against God.

God has not fallen because Jerusalem has; His righteousness and His truth are not darkened because of the black evil of the present. The Hebrews are suffering now because they are worse than the others in that they knew God and turned from His righteousness, but all the other nations shall be punished in like measure and shall learn by the fury of His wrath that this God of a shamed and enslaved people is the Lord God of heaven and earth "who shall be sanctified before the eyes of the heathen," and who shall preserve His people Israel when their conquerors have passed away forever. No dream could have seemed more baseless and unreal, but no prophecy was ever more literally fulfilled. The man who spoke it had a great share in bringing it to pass.

That spirit of unshaken confidence in the ultimate strength of the good no matter how strong the immediate evil is, marked every one of the prophets. There Ezekiel saw exactly as the men before him did. But oftenest he differed from them and always to his mental and spiritual disadvantage. Marvels are remarkable by their absence from the other books. Isaiah indeed had once had a vision of wondrous beings attendant upon God, but there is nothing else of the kind in his book or anywhere in the other early prophets except in Ezekiel. He is given over to that sort of thing to such a degree that whole chapters of his book seem to belong not to the Old Testament, but to the world of Oriental fantasy and magic, so foreign and hateful, for the most part, to the Hebrew writers. He was perpetually visited by the most extraordinary visions. Only a very determined and exceptionally ingenious symbolist can do anything with them. Stupendous forms appear to him having many heads, human and animal, shaped like men, but with hoofs instead of feet and "their whole body full of eyes round about," while "as for their rings [whatever that may mean] they were so high that they were dreadful." These singular creatures are found in the first chapter and they keep on recurring in the midst of the fiery indictments of sin which are Ezekiel's main subject, with as surprising an effect as if one came upon an account of hobgoblins in a prayer book.

Visions belong especially to lonely men. Ezekiel was an exile in Chaldea. He was one of the band carried to Babylon before the fall of Jerusalem, which Jeremiah says was made up of the king and nobles and skilled workmen, and he himself says that he had been there nearly thirteen years when "one that had escaped out of Jerusalem came unto me saying, The city is smitten." On nearly every page of his book are touches that show his loneliness and his homesickness. The strange country he found himself in was "a dry and thirsty ground," above which "the terrible crystal stretched forth over their heads," the fearful burning sky of Southern Asia. There he, a hillsman, was to spend the rest of his life. In his thoughts, turned ever toward his home, little craggy Palestine became transformed into a land of great mountains and rushing rivers, a land fresh and green, "like a vine planted by the waters and full of branches by reason of many waters." No other book in the Bible has anything like so much about hills and valleys and shade trees and water; one might almost say all the other books together have not. "The mountains of Israel"—over and over again he repeats the phrase. Trees he is forever bringing in, "green trees and thick oaks"; "cedars of Lebanon with thick branches," "their roots by great waters"; fir trees and chestnut trees and willows "with thick boughs that drink water"; "a goodly cedar and in the shadow of the branches thereof dwelt all birds of every wing"; "trees fairer than any tree in the garden of God." Water is even more in his mind. Of course the canals of the Euphrates were there for him. The little town he lived in, near Babylon, was beside one of them. Babylon itself was far from a dry and thirsty city. But ditches full of a brown sluggish liquid were not what he meant by water. He saw in his mind clear, leaping hillside streams, "a multitude of waters and great waters," "running rivers and little rivers that go to every tree of the field"; "the mountains of Israel by the rivers." The dream city he builds in his last chapters is on a mountain where waters rush forth, deepening until they are "waters to swim in," on whose banks are "very many trees on the one side and on the other."

These vivid phrases are little flashing pictures of his own mind so far as his longing for home is concerned and his detestation of the land of his exile; but this is practically all that he gives us of himself and it does not take us very far. He never speaks directly of what he felt about anything.

When his wife died the only indication of what he suffered is God's statement, "Behold I take away from thee the desire of thine eyes." "And at even my wife died," he concludes, and that is all. Nothing really of what he himself was comes through. He stays aloof, remote. He never says anything against Chaldea, except by inference, and, still more surprising, he never says anything at all about Babylon.

Strange people surrounded him; in his ears, he says, was "a strange speech and a hard language"; strange customs must often have offended him, horrified him. He did not let one word of what he felt escape him. Strange sights filled his eyes wherever he went; he never speaks of these either. One cannot help conjecturing that the portentous visions he had were suggested to him by monstrous fantasies of decoration and prodigious gods he saw as he walked in court and street; but this again is only an inference. He tells us nothing even indirectly about what is called in the book of Isaiah "the golden city, Babylon, the glory of kingdoms, the beauty of the Chaldeans' excellency." Strangest of all, he never speaks of the exiled Hebrews' sufferings or so much as hints at any blame of their masters.

Back of this silence must have lain a deliberate policy. Jeremiah had urged upon the Babylonian captives complete submission. He had written them to be the faithful and obedient servants of their conquerors. Ezekiel was one of those to whom the letter was addressed, and it seems clear that he recognized the wisdom of the advice. He saw that it pointed out the only way which gave the Hebrews a chance of surviving and he determined to do as the great teacher directed: he would avoid even any word that could cause irritation. Therefore he kept silent. He saw nothing to praise, or, at the least, there was nothing he was willing to praise.

But it is a curious circumstance that the one part of his book which gives us a vivid picture of that remote, strange world, is a detailed and glowing description of the commerce of Tyre. To be sure, that city was much in men's minds just then because of the long siege of her by Nebuchadnezzar which lasted for thirteen years, but that is no reason why Ezekiel should wander away into an enthusiastic account of the treasures that were bought and sold in her. They have nothing to do with his only purpose in writing about her, to declare that the Chaldeans will certainly destroy her because of her wickedness, but he loses sight of any and every point in his wondering delight at the splendors he seems to see heaped up in her streets. Why in Tyre and not in Babylon? It would seem improbable that Ezekiel was ever in Tyre; even if in his early youth he had made a visit there, his descriptions are not those of sights seen long ago; what he writes of is unmistakably before his eyes. Why Tyre then? She was no longer queen of commerce as she had been in Isaiah's day when her merchants were princes and her traffickers the honorable of the earth. Under Nebuchadnezzar Babylon had supplanted her. It was in the streets of Babylon that Ezekiel saw what he transferred to Tyre because he would not seem to admire the hated city—and how he admired what he saw in her! The interest for buying and selling which was to mark his race, and their love for the completed product of men's work, can be felt throughout this long and curious excursion into the costly objects of luxury flowing from everywhere in the world to the mistress of the world. All nations known to man, Ezekiel declares, "were thy merchants by reason of the multitude of the wares of thy making," at "great fairs where thy merchants trade in a multitude of all kinds of riches."

He lingers lovingly over each beautiful and precious thing, "fine linen with broidered work from Egypt"; "blue and purple from the isles"; "vessels of brass" brought by "traders from the sea"; "wine and white wool from Damascus"; "spices and gold" from Sheba; "chariots and precious clothes for chariots"; "ebony and horns of ivory"; jewels, "every precious stone, the sardius, topaz, and the diamond; the beryl, the onyx, and the jasper; the sapphire, the emerald, and the carbuncle," with "coral and agate from Sheba and from Syria." "Blue clothes," too, and "chests of rich apparel bound with cords and made of cedar," from nations that have no place any more on earth.

And Greece—her first appearance in the Bible except for one allusion, probably a late addition, in Genesis—"traded the persons of men in thy market." An ignoble entry for her into world commerce, but she was closely connected with the slave-trade, the prophet Joel declares, buying as well as selling: "The children of Jerusalem have ye (Tyre and Sidon) sold unto the Grecians."

These chapters strike a new note in the Old Testament. Luxuries are absent up to this point, except for the blaze of gold in Solomon's temple. Amos cites only one among the extravagances of the wicked rich, "beds of ivory"—his "houses of ivory" must have been a current phrase for very white houses. For the rest he describes the excesses of landed proprietors who can afford to eat the young of their flocks and herds and "drink wine from bowls." To Hosea and Micah too wealth is "abundance of corn and wine and oil," and the same is really true of Isaiah in spite of his fine ladies' clothes and in spite of the fact that he was a city man as the other three were not. He says once indeed that the land is full of silver and gold and "treasures," but on nearly every page of his book there are pastoral allusions that call up country riches: people are gleaning grapes and shaking down olives and harvesting ears of corn and singing as they tread out the wine. Jerusalem is "a lodge in a garden of cucumbers," or, oftenest, she is God's vineyard:

Now will I sing to my well beloved
A song of my beloved touching his vineyard. . . .
He fenced it and gathered out the stones thereof . . .
And he looked that it should bring forth grapes,
And it brought forth wild grapes.

Jeremiah, a hundred years later, saw even less extravagant display than Isaiah, but it would be rash to conclude that there was therefore less in his day. He was never a man to notice women's clothes. In Egypt, too, all the magnificence around him passed him by. He did not give a thought to it; he had not Ezekiel's eye.

Luxury, full grown, and commerce of an Oriental richness and splendor make their first appearance in Ezekiel, foreshadowing the destiny of his race. The Hebrews' future share in the work of the world is to be seen in these chapters. In the countries to which they would wander they were fated to find themselves shut out from any share in the land, forced to give up the pastoral life they had lived for unnumbered years. They were to be not creators of wealth as in a humble way they had always been, but distributors, especially of beautiful and costly objects like those that so stirred Ezekiel to admiration. They were to be the purveyors to the world of the superfluities of life, in most singular contrast to the setting and the spirit of their literature.

But if the book of Ezekiel, apart from its wholesale denunciations of mankind in general, did no more than paint the loneliness and homesickness of the exiles and suggest the first dawning of the commercial instinct in them, it would be negligible today. On the contrary, it is a very important document. It is the earliest record we have of the way the most powerful form of organization is developed, religious organization. Ezekiel is the first religious organizer we know about and the greatest. Others there were before him who must have had first-rate ability. The priesthoods of Egypt and Chaldea were powers kings bowed down before. But they passed, leaving hardly a trace behind them. The organization Ezekiel started has resisted the changes not of centuries but of millennia.

It was he who laid down the lines along which the Hebrews were enabled to remain Hebrews although millennia were to pass before they again became an independent people. When Jerusalem fell freedom ended for them. A little nation, quite insignificant politically, neither strong nor rich, was conquered; her capital razed to the ground; her population enslaved and in large part carried off to the country of her conquerors. It would seem past belief that she could keep her identity, a handful of helpless captives in the midst of the ruling power of the world. One would suppose them foredoomed to disintegrate and disappear. That is what happened to the other nations that went down under Nineveh and Babylon, often great and powerful nations, the Ammonites, the Moabites, the Phoenicians, and many another. They and the two mighty cities that conquered them have no place in our world today except in the libraries. Nor was Israel, carried to Assyria a hundred years or so before the fall of Jerusalem, able to maintain herself. The ten tribes vanished; of the Israelites left in their country there is no record; we know nothing whatever about them. But when Judah finally went back from Chaldea to Palestine, what returned was the same that had gone away.

It is not possible to say why Israel reacted so differently. The only difference now visible in her situation is that she was conquered a hundred years earlier and that Nineveh was cruel as Babylon was not. It is hardly credible that all her brilliant literary activity should at once have come to an end, but if after her capture there were any prophets like the Israelite Hosea comforting and sustaining her people in their misery, any writers like her early historians pointing out that God was accomplishing His purpose through their pain, not one word has come down to us. Israel disappeared from the Bible. The wonder is that Judah kept her place. A tremendous force operated to bring about her survival and it was set to work by Ezekiel.

He was a priest, the only one of the prophets who was, except Jeremiah. Priest and prophet do not go well together. In Jeremiah's case the prophet very early drove the priest out; with Ezekiel it was the other way about.

The Hebrew prophets were men possessed by the idea that what ought to be can and must be brought to pass. Their only aim was to establish on earth the rule of justice and mercy; their only method of doing this was to induce men to become just and merciful. Isaiah and Jeremiah, for all their longing that Jerusalem should be saved, are still within that category. They both believed that the Hebrews were not worth saving unless they lived as the God of righteousness would have them. Authority meant nothing to any of them, except the authority of God, which speaks through the conscience. Authority as it is usually understood, they had no use for. It could not produce or assist in producing a just and merciful man. They never dreamed of organizing to make their ideas effective. Whether they had any ability along that line or not they certainly had no interest. Their attention was fixed upon the conscience, which is very poor material to build an organization upon, of all human things the most stubbornly individual, the least submissive to authority.

But the priest in every age stands first of all for authority because he stands for organization. The two are interdependent; neither can exist without the other in any big and impressive way. Ezekiel had the priestly temper of mind. He was a man of genius and he became a supreme organizer. The institution which grew up on the foundation he laid is the oldest in our world today; it has lasted for more than two thousand five hundred years.

With all of his dreams and visions he was exceedingly practical. The combination is not as unusual as it may seem at first sight, and it results in a tremendously effective personality, one with the absolute certainty that takes possession of a man convinced that he has actually seen the truth, and at the same time with the ability to make the truth work efficiently. St. Paul was like that and so was St. Augustine. Luther is an example too and Mahomet supremely so. These men were triumphantly successful organizers. But Ezekiel was the forerunner and his methods were followed, consciously or unconsciously, by them all. He is the model organizer of religion.

Amos, Isaiah, and the rest had nothing of that sort of efficiency. It is true that they were far removed from being dreamers or mere theorists. They were realists whose eyes were fixed upon the actual human life around them and whose one concern was to make it better. They cared only for what had value for daily living. But their idea of what was valuable was limited to one thing, to act according to the righteous will of God. All that went counter to this in the slightest respect they rejected, no matter what it promised of immediate relief or improvement.

The world they lived in was brutal and cruel almost past our power to imagine. On Assyrian bas-reliefs soldiers play ball with severed heads; kings stand beside heaps of ears, arms, legs, torn from their captives, to their contemporaries a glory for them to boast of. And yet the prophets would allow no aim except to establish in that world the reign of justice and mercy. They would have nothing to do with any lesser good. That would be to lower the service of God and in the end to lower God Himself. He demanded of men a justice not qualified, a mercy not limited, but perfect and never deviated from, and what God required man could do. He did not ask impossibilities; indeed, His requirements were the measure of man's power. Therefore the rule of justice and mercy was possible here and now, and nothing else was of any value at all.

But the terrible present pressed upon Ezekiel. He was in exile, his ruined countrymen around him; he faced the imminent peril of God's people being obliterated, becoming one with their conquerors. Amos and Isaiah would have said that even so, God's work alone must be done with a single purpose; but to Ezekiel, agonized to save the broken nation, which was, after all, the only one that knew God, this would have seemed a senseless refusal to look facts in the face. It was not that he did not believe in justice and mercy. He really believed that they and those who practiced them were safe in the hands of the just and merciful God. But in this terrible crisis, this instant danger, it was impossible that they should be enough; he could not depend on them alone. Certainly by themselves they would not preserve the Hebrew nation. And it must be preserved. That was the matter of first importance at the moment. Justice and mercy must come second. Somehow, the deadly process of growing friendliness to the Chaldeans through sharing common interests with them must be blocked. The nation must be bound indissolubly together in such a way as to separate them conspicuously from all others. They must be set apart once and for all, divided from their next-door neighbor, so to speak, from those they were living beside, growing accustomed to, learning to understand. It was a tremendous undertaking and it was purely experimental. It had never been attempted before.

He was perfectly right as he saw the situation. He could not trust to justice and mercy alone; they would never have kept the Hebrews a distinct people. They are not dividing forces; they bring men together. What separates is the sense of superiority, of the clique, the caste, the race, and its correlative, the sense of inferiority. "The Brahman and the pariah, the dreaded and the despised," says India, the land of divisions. Every other barrier between men can be passed; this alone is insurmountable. Eliminate it and the distinctions that remain do not work for separation. Natural differences of themselves are not barriers, even the greatest differences in power of mind or spirit. The poet, artist, scientist, never arouse the feeling of inferiority in the rest of us. Their genius is our possession. Actual superiority is the most unifying force in the world. It brings understanding, which means feeling with others, and disinterestedness, which means putting others first.

But the consciousness of being set above others because one has blue blood or a white skin or the correct method of preparing food or the unique knowledge of the truth is the great disrupting force, and so Ezekiel saw. He called it in to help him in the task he had set himself and it did not fail him. This is, of course, an inference only. There is no statement to that effect in his book. The prophets were not given to stating in clear terms their program. But it is an inevitable inference from the difference between his teaching and that of the men before him. Even in that book of ritual, Deuteronomy, there is no direct reference to the rite of circumcision. Amos, Isaiah, and the rest, it goes without saying, completely ignore it. Ezekiel emphasizes it far and away beyond any other book in the Old Testament. Only the circumcised can enter God's sanctuary. If the uncircumcised so much as cross the threshold they will "pollute" it. In verse after verse he scorns them! "Yea, thou shalt be broken in the midst of the uncircumcised"; "And they lie uncircumcised . . . and bear their shame with them that go down to the pit." So, too, keeping the Sabbath, which Isaiah had denounced and none of his three fellow seers had urged or even mentioned, Ezekiel preaches the necessity of in the eyes of God. God says: "Hallow my sabbaths and they shall be a sign between me and you that I am the Lord your God." In one chapter and another He denounces those that have "profaned my sabbaths"; He declares, "They polluted my sabbaths: then I said I would pour out my fury upon them."

It is not so clear that Ezekiel perceived the full value for his purpose of another ancient Hebrew custom in killing animals to be used as food. Still he speaks of meat not so prepared as "abominable flesh" and denounces them that "eat with blood," that is, eat what is not ritually correct. Needless to say, no prophet before him had ever referred to this practice, let alone recommended it as a way to please God. Jeremiah in Egypt had no thought to bid his countrymen do anything that would divide them from the Egyptians save only not give to idols what was due to the Almighty God.

But Ezekiel had the spirit of the ritualist. There was a whole class of acts which were "holy" and "clean" without having any bearing whatsoever upon life. Priests wore "holy garments" and kept them in "holy chambers" and ate "most holy things." "And they shall teach my people the difference between the holy and the profane, and cause them to discern between the clean and the unclean"—among the former being a certain kind of dress and a certain style of wearing the hair. "Wash you, make you clean," said Isaiah, "cease to do evil . . . relieve the oppressed, judge the fatherless, plead for the widow."

One verse in Ezekiel gives to perfection the ritualistic scale of values. God is represented as declaring that "they have defiled my sanctuary. For when they had slain their children to their idols, then they came the same day into my sanctuary to profane it." The importance of the unreal above the real is as clear in this verse as in that familiar statement of triumphant ritual when they took Christ to Pilate "and they themselves went not into the judgment hall lest they should be defiled." So with the same scale of values the Crusaders on their way to deliver the "holy" sepulcher tortured and massacred the Jews of Europe.

It is clear that of the three customs chosen out by Ezekiel neither circumcision nor preparing food according to a prescribed ritual was to be practiced because it had value for life. The fact that circumcision is approved today has no bearing here. It was not regarded as hygienic but purely as an all-important rite. The Hebrew mind, with its intuitive feeling for the permanently real, was rejecting Amos' and Isaiah's realism to emphasize the unreal. These customs had no value in helping men to make their lives better. In another sense, however, they were emphatically real: they were admirable separators. Merely as a term of reproach "the uncircumcised" had great potentialities along that line. Names have been very important factors in separating people. And, of course, to have a sacred custom which made it impossible to eat with others was a hardly to be surpassed bar to friendliness.

The Sabbath as a day of rest for toiling men is on another level; it is altogether beneficial. So much so that it would tend to commend itself as reasonable and merciful. Such a custom, so truly superior, would not arouse permanent antagonism; it would end by making converts. But as Ezekiel preached it and as it grew holier and holier, it became precisely what Isaiah had denounced, a day of bondage to exacting ceremonial rules, which, however valued by those brought up in its tradition, could not possibly attract men in general as a force for good. The effect of it was finally as great as that of the other two in cutting the Hebrews off from natural, friendly intercourse with everyone not a Hebrew.

These were all practices old and dear to the people and no doubt along with every national custom especially precious to them in their exile. In a sense Ezekiel's foundation was ready laid for him. What he did was to focus the attention upon the regulations that were most conspicuously Hebrew and so simplify the issue for the mass of the people. He gave them too a title and a slogan. They were the Circumcised and they alone knew what was clean and unclean, holy and profane. He had the authority of the greatest men of his race against him as he insisted on the overwhelming importance to God of precisely what his predecessors and his contemporary, Jeremiah, had declared God despised and hated. It would seem, indeed, from Jeremiah's account that these teachings had had very little effect, and yet there is the significant fact that they had been preserved for nearly two hundred years, handed down from one generation to another as spoken by men of God. Nevertheless, it is impossible to believe that Ezekiel found them any real obstacle. When a series of statements is traditionally sacred and continually repeated, directly opposed ideas can be expressed at the same time with wonderful ease to the hearers. No doubt the Hebrews listened quite comfortably to Isaiah's declaration that God's soul hated the Sabbath and Jeremiah's scornful question, "Can scraps of fat and sacred flesh avert calamity?", while approving Ezekiel's directions for pleasing God by holy Sabbath offerings and for escaping the calamity of God's anger by sacrificing fat and sacred flesh.

Above all, Ezekiel was backed by the delightful persuasion of exclusive superiority. All the weight of the great prophets could not hold that down. As Ezekiel preached it, the little band of captives ceased to be hopeless, humiliated slaves. They were given an exhilarating and fortifying sense of being lifted above their conquerors and banded together against them. The foundation for that triumph of exclusiveness, the organization of the Jewish people, was almost complete.

But if there had been no more to it than that, it would not have endured. An organization which has nothing in it to satisfy some higher aim and longing in men cannot last as Ezekiel's lasted. If it seeks only to perpetuate a certain division, whether of race or class or conviction, it will pass away. Mankind in the long run insists on more than that. This truth could not escape Ezekiel, the Hebrew. It was his birthright to understand the longing for God in the human heart. From earliest childhood he had been taught that man doth not live by bread alone; there was a Hebrew proverb, a familiar saying of universal acceptance, that "where there is no vision the people perish." He turned back to ritual indeed, but he took over righteousness as well. Hosea's mercy and not sacrifice became for him mercy and also sacrifice. God's anger was as hot against those "who have vexed the poor and the needy and have oppressed the stranger," as it was against the uncircumcised and those who "eat with blood." He would smite those who "greedily gain of their neighbors by extortion" along with those who "profane my sabbaths."

There lay the peculiar strength of what he was attempting, religious organization. It could combine opposites. It could appeal at the same time to the desire of being superior to others and to the inner imperative of human sympathy, to selfishness and to unselfishness. It could sustain the best in men as well as the poorest.

Century after century has proved the strength of this combination, in many forms, over all the world. As Ezekiel shaped it, it has endured storms such as have visited no other. The history of the Jewish people is one long record of terror and agony, but after two thousand years of unparalleled suffering their organization still appears indestructible. That is primarily Ezekiel's achievement, and beside it the empires and the conquests of the heroes of history seem impermanent superficialities.

But no one can consider it without wondering what would have happened if he too had believed that only justice and mercy mattered, and if his people had followed him there as on the path to God. Isaiah and Micah and Jeremiah, so believing, had had a vision of what divides men ceasing to be. They had seen not a separated Hebrew nation who were the favorites of God, but "All the nations gathered to the name of the Lord," "All nations flowing to the mountain of the Lord's house," when the Lord would say, "Blessed be Egypt, my people, and Assyria, the work of my hands." Then, Jeremiah said, there would be an end to the cause of divisions, to superior possession of holy things or holy knowledge, even to that Holy of Holies, the ark, God's earthly throne: "In

those days, saith the Lord, they shall say no more
the ark of the covenant, neither shall they remember it." Then, Isaiah and Micah said, there would
be an end to the result of divisions: "Nation shall
not lift up sword against nation, neither shall they
learn war any more, and none shall make them
afraid."

Instead, Ezekiel left behind him an ever inten-
sifying cause for dividing man from man and a
never ending result of the cruelty and the anguish
men divided against each other always bring
about.

Blessed is the man that feareth the Lord, that delighteth greatly in his commandments. His seed shall be mighty upon the earth: the generation of the upright shall be blessed. Wealth and riches shall be in his house.

Psalms 112:1, 2, 3

Both riches and honour come of thee.

I Chronicles 29:12

CHAPTER X

As It Was in
the Beginning—

❖ ❖ ❖ ❖ ❖ ❖ ❖ ❖ ❖ ❖ ❖ ❖ ❖ ❖ ❖ ❖ ❖ ❖ ❖

AMOS, MICAH, ISAIAH, all appeared in little more than one generation, three men who preached the same new doctrines with extraordinary power, claiming to be the spokesmen of God, invested with His authority, their discourse prefaced and punctuated with "Thus saith the Lord." New doctrines are always unpopular, more or less; among theirs was one which was emphatically more. In point of fact, it was the most unpopular ever preached and whenever in later centuries the prophets' words fired others to take it up, it aroused a determined and persistent antagonism which proved invariably able to silence its champions.

The prophets taught that God was for the poor

and the weak and against the rich and the powerful. Wealth they said, in effect, was always the
result of injustice. In Amos it is only another term
for wickedness. Isaiah and Micah, who agree with
him, put the aristocrats in the same class. The
nobles and the princes are just as bad as "the rich
man full of violence"; "companions of thieves"
Isaiah calls them, while Micah says that "they
eat the flesh of my people." The poor, on the contrary, are the peculiar charge of God. He is their
strength in their distress; their refuge from the
storm.

These ideas preached with the immense fire and
passion of the prophets must have been exceedingly disturbing to the men of property and
authority. Of course they could assure themselves
that there never had been an uprising of the poor.
There could be no reason to fear anything like
that. How could the powerless rebel? And yet it
can hardly be doubted that Isaiah, at least, so well
known and so distinguished, the counselor of
kings, could not speak such words without causing some stir in the lower depths, arousing some
hope among the hopeless. Certainly the rich and
ruling classes would have been unlike their kind
at all times everywhere if they had not been quick
to take alarm and adopt repressive measures. The
priests as always were in close alliance with them,
in this case for specially good reasons. None of

the prophets ever had anything to say for the priesthood. Every church and every state under such circumstances would agree that they must make an end of the subversive notion that the poor were not in the world for the rich to dispose of, but that they had rights in the eyes of God.

We cannot trace the steps the guardians of law and order took. They left no record of their agitated and indignant consultations. But that bit of history has been repeated so often, it is the easiest thing in the world to reconstruct it. An attack on private property! The fruits of a man's honest labor no longer secure for him! Men who had made the prosperity of the country vilified, and lazy incompetents, the dregs of the populace, encouraged to assert themselves. Pernicious ideas abroad and resolute action necessary. We shall never know whose was the keen mind that suggested, Back to Moses. All that the Hebrew chroniclers tell us is the discovery of a book. Perhaps fifty years after Isaiah's death the temple was being repaired and the high priest sent a scroll to the king with the message that he had found it in the temple and that it was "a book of the law of the Lord given by Moses." The king received it with reverence and summoning "all the people, great and small," he read to them "all the words of the book."

That scroll is now believed to have been the

Book of Deuteronomy, composed by the priests shortly before it was ostensibly discovered. Every word of it purports to have come from Moses. It would be hard to imagine anything better calculated to nullify the prophets' revolutionary creed. The fundamental doctrine it teaches is that prosperity and riches come to the good as a reward from God, and that poverty and misfortune are the punishment for doing wrong. This was an ancient belief which in its essentials the Hebrews shared with all the other peoples of the earth. When the prophets attacked it they set themselves against an idea that was basic in the thought of the times. When they declared that to be poor and wretched was not the result of God's anger, but the passport to His favor, they were turning the world upside down. In Deuteronomy the priests restored the balance and ensured its stability.

This old and honored doctrine that to obey God is the way to security and ease and to disobey Him the way to calamity is expressed throughout the book with simple directness: "Thou shalt remember the Lord thy God: for it is he that giveth thee power to get wealth. . . . If thou hearken diligently unto the voice of the Lord thy God . . . the Lord shall command the blessing upon thee in thy store-houses . . . and make thee plenteous in goods. But if thou wilt not hearken unto the voice of the Lord . . . thou shalt serve in hunger

and in thirst and in nakedness." No other motive
for doing right is ever held out. There are no such
tremendous curses anywhere else in literature as
those Moses rolls forth against men that do not
do God's commandments. They shall be cursed
in the city and cursed in the field. The fruit of
their body shall be cursed, the fruit of their land,
the increase of their kine and the flocks of their
sheep. The heaven that is over them shall be brass
and the earth that is under them shall be iron.
In the morning they shall say, Would God it were
even! And at even they shall say, Would God it
were morning! The blessings on the good are much
less impressive; still they are all that could be desired. The Lord will bless them and their land,
their corn, their wine, their oil, and the flocks of
their sheep.

The book is magnificently written. Great men
were its authors, only not great enough to see
farther than their own interests and to work with
the prophets for a new world and a new conception of the justice of God. But even so, the God
in their pages is grandly conceived. There are
descriptions of Him that match any in the Bible,
sometimes so beautifully tender as to recall, not
quite Hosea, but the best in Micah and Isaiah:

> The eternal God is thy refuge.
> And underneath are the everlasting arms—

Love and compassion belong to the God of Deuteronomy—along with a good deal else. He will
punish most horribly, but He will love and pity
too. He executes judgment for the fatherless and
widow; He defends the stranger—a contradiction,
of course, to the main thesis of the book, but the
authors were not prepared to follow it to its logical
conclusion. They were helped out in their general
reasoning by the assertion in the Ten Commandments that although God did show mercy to those
that kept His commandments, nevertheless He
visited the sins of the fathers upon the children.
There the Hebrew sense for fact came in. They
never were able to close their eyes comfortably
to things as they are. Good people did suffer, but
there was a reason. Children suffering for their
fathers' sins did not offend their notion of justice
as it does ours, and as, indeed, it did offend
both Jeremiah's and Ezekiel's, who both protested
against believing that God approved such an idea.
But except for a few super-men the individual as
yet hardly existed. Fathers and sons were not
really to be distinguished. Hosea's conception of
God, however, was more than a hundred years
old when Deuteronomy was written, and the most
rigidly logical priest would not by then have maintained that widows and orphans had in the eyes
of God got only what they deserved.

Nor did the authors of the book fail to emphasize the mercy and the compassion of God. They held Him up to be feared, certainly, but certainly too to be loved: "Hear, O Israel, the Lord our God, the Lord is one. And thou shalt love the Lord thy God with all thine heart and with all thy soul and with all thy might."

In such passages the authors reach a level as high as that of any part of the Old Testament except the prophets at their highest. And in one remarkable verse the wanderings in the wilderness are described not as God's punishment, but as His means of teaching. The Lord caused them "that he might make thee know that man doth not live by bread only, but by every word that proceedeth out of the mouth of the Lord . . . that as a man chasteneth his son, so the Lord thy God chasteneth thee." Whoever wrote that had caught a glimpse of a new idea of suffering.

But everywhere else the lesson is driven home that men suffer only because God is angry with them. The book is addressed entirely to the non-sufferers, to those with "goodly houses" and vineyards and flocks and herds and slaves. Not a word is addressed to the slaves themselves or to the poor. It is assumed that they are to be at the disposal of the rich.

Under these conditions, the authors show themselves kind and conscientious men in urging a liberal charity—within bounds. There must be no idea of getting rid of poverty: "For the poor shall never cease out of the land." But once this fact was clearly recognized [did cheap labor play a part?], they went on to say: "Thou shalt open thine hand wide . . . to thy poor and to thy needy in thy land."

Of course with the priestly authorship, the prophets' denunciations of ritual were completely passed over. The book indeed declares repeatedly, not only that God desires sacrifices, but that He will accept only those offered at Jerusalem by the temple priests. The writers here, indeed, faced a real problem. Moses in the desert could hardly tell the people that they must go to a city which did not yet exist and give their offerings to priests of a building which was not yet built, but the difficulty is skilfully evaded. When the promised land is reached, Moses declares, God will choose a place to cause His name to dwell there, and thither shall all offerings be brought. At this point the priests, experienced in the way an audience can forget what they have just been told, felt it advisable to recall the situation to their hearers, and Moses tells the Israelites, who by hypothesis are listening to him "in the wilderness over against the Red Sea," not to forget that they have not yet reached that land of promise or that Jordan's crossing still lies before them.

There are a number of similar indications of

the late date of the book and who were the authors, and in general the observances emphasized are those that bear the unmistakable mark of priestly ritual, impressive because of the very lack of common sense which, it seems, must point to some deep, mysterious meaning: "Thou shalt not wear a garment of woolen and linen together." Church and state would never be endangered by such injunctions. Were they, perhaps, the priests' retort to Micah's "What doth the Lord require of thee, but to do justly, and to love mercy, and to walk humbly with thy God?"

Far and away beyond all the rest, however, the book was calculated to carry a conviction of the moral superiority of the prosperous and inferiority of the unfortunate. Against ideas so comfortable to the men of substance how could a gospel for the poor spread? Deuteronomy became at once the book of books in the Hebrew religion.

To a nation trained in this economic view of the origin of wealth, and in this philosophy of the meaning of suffering, came the fall of Jerusalem and the Exile.

They that sow in tears shall reap in joy.

Psalms 126:5

For the earth shall be filled with the knowledge of the
glory of the Lord, as the waters cover the sea.

Habakkuk 2:14

CHAPTER XI

The Exile and the
Second Isaiah

❖ ❖ ❖ ❖ ❖ ❖ ❖ ❖ ❖ ❖ ❖ ❖ ❖ ❖ ❖ ❖ ❖ ❖ ❖

By the rivers of Babylon,
There we sat down, yea, we wept
When we remembered Zion. . . .
For they that carried us away captive required of us
    a song. . . .
How shall we sing the Lord's song
In a strange land?
If I forget thee, O Jerusalem,
Let my right hand forget her cunning. . . .
O daughter of Babylon . . .
Happy shall he be that rewardeth thee
As thou hast served us.
Happy shall he be that taketh and dasheth thy little
    ones
Against the stones.

    Something of what the Hebrews felt during the
Exile, how they suffered and how they hated when

(209)

Jerusalem had fallen and they were captives in Chaldea, can be seen here and there in the Psalms. Their shame and despair in slavery and the fury of their helpless anger, which Jeremiah had forbidden them ever to show and which Ezekiel had not allowed himself to speak of or even hint at, is expressed by one psalmist and another:

O God, the heathen are come into thine inheritance;
They have defiled thy holy temple;
They have made Jerusalem into heaps. . . .
We are become a taunt to our neighbors,
A scorn and derision to them that are round about us.

Often only a single sentence or even a phrase brings vividly to mind the anguish of those years: Out of the depths have I cried unto thee, O Lord— Let the sighing of the prisoner come before thee — Thou feedest thy people with the bread of tears and givest them tears to drink in great measure— How long, O Lord.

Through their agony of sorrow their passionate anger breaks out:

O Lord God to whom vengeance belongeth;
O God to whom vengeance belongeth, show thyself.
Lift up thyself, thou judge of the earth:
Render to the proud their recompense.
Lord, how long shall the wicked,
How long shall the wicked triumph?

But poignant and burning though these words are, the men who wrote them did not sound the deepest depths of the nation's pain. The Hebrews were looking at a horror: it seemed that God had failed. "The faithful God" of Deuteronomy, "which keepeth covenant," appeared to have faithlessly broken His covenant. Seven hundred miles stretched from Jerusalem to Babylon. As the defeated soldiers plodded on through heat and dust and thirst, the men who had fought so fiercely and so resolutely for their city which was God's city, as each day brought them nearer to slavery, they must have thought much about the Lord their God. Deuteronomy had been their Bible, the words of Moses, the man of God, which God Himself had put into his mouth. It was true that he had declared God would punish His people terribly if they forsook Him, and there could be no doubt that many of them had done that very thing. Sunworship had been carried on in the temple itself; women had burned incense to the queen of heaven openly, in the streets. Jeremiah's thunder must still have echoed in their ears. They acknowledged that they deserved to suffer. And yet the triumphant Chaldeans were all out-and-out idolaters; shameful practices went on in their temples; they were beyond comparison worse than the Hebrews. Was their conquest the work of a just God? Once arrived in Babylon the captives must have seen every day the superiority of their own faith and morality to that around them. They had believed with complete confidence that God visited wickedness with fearful calamities. Not in Babylon, it seemed, but only in Judaea.

Ezekiel could declare that it was right for them to be judged more sternly than others because they had been taught by God and knew better. As Amos had said: "You only have I known of all the families of the earth: therefore I will punish you for all your iniquities." But this was a doctrine for the very strong only. Few could find in it the means of holding to their faith in the God Who had promised to keep His covenant that the bad should never prosper.

The problem of evil confronted the Hebrews inescapably in Babylon. Even before Jerusalem fell two men had puzzled over it. Jeremiah and his contemporary, the prophet Habakkuk, both perceived that the facts of experience were at odds with the thesis of Deuteronomy. Jeremiah ventured a remonstrance: "Righteous art thou, O Lord, when I plead with thee, yet let me talk with thee of thy judgments: wherefore doth the way of the wicked prosper? Wherefore are they happy that deal very treacherously?" Habakkuk went further, pointing out to God that He was contradicting Himself when He did not defend the good: "Thou art of purer eyes than to behold iniquity:

wherefore lookest thou upon them that deal
treacherously and holdest thy tongue when the
wicked devoureth the man that is more righteous
than he?" But neither man found any real answer.
Habakkuk's is only an assertion that the triumph
of the wicked shall be short-lived; Jeremiah's,
which is that children do suffer from their fathers'
sins, but nevertheless receive from God only the
just reward of what they do themselves, must have
cost his great intellect a struggle. "Ah Lord God!
Behold . . . there is nothing too hard for thee.
Thou shewest lovingkindness unto thousands, and
recompensest the iniquity of the fathers into the
bosom of their children after them: the Great, the
Mighty God, the Lord of hosts, is his name, great
in counsel and mighty in work: for thine eyes are
open upon all the ways of the sons of men: to
give every one according to his ways and according to the fruit of his doing."

But the Exile forced a sterner logic. Three
tendencies, all poles apart, began to show themselves. One was the effort to lift the charge of
injustice from God by shouldering a burden of sin
too great for forgiveness. The milder and submissive spirits turned their eyes upon themselves to
seek within their hearts evil black enough to
justify their sufferings. The Book of Lamentations
which was, at any rate on the face of it, written
around this time shows best this attitude:

Is it nothing to you, all ye that pass by?
Behold, and see
If there be any sorrow like unto my sorrow,
Wherewith the Lord hath afflicted me
In the day of his fierce anger. . . .
The Lord is righteous;
For I have rebelled against his commandment.

And again, hardly in submission, but in stern acquiescence:

I am the man that hath seen affliction
By the rod of his wrath.
He hath led me and caused me to walk
In darkness and not in light. . . .
Wherefore doth a living man complain,
A man for the punishment of his sins?

Some of the psalms, too, which are held to belong to this period, show how heavily the conviction of sin weighed:

For I acknowledge my transgression and my sin is
ever before me.

And then the completely illogical and touchingly loyal conclusion:

Against thee, thee only have I sinned . . .
That thou mightest be justified . . . ,
And be clear when thou judgest.

But there were others who were not submissive. The cruder spirits among them proclaimed vociferously their righteousness. The psalms they wrote read like a scream to God to attend to what is happening and rouse Himself to defend the righteous, of whom the psalmist is always one. The Cursing Psalms these compositions are called and they are remarkable productions, hymns of hate, fierce requests for vengeance to a God as fierce and revengeful: "Let their (the psalmist's) enemies' eyes be darkened that they see not. . . . Pour out thine indignation upon them, and let thy wrathful anger take hold of them. Let their habitation be desolate and let none dwell in their tents. . . . Let them be blotted out of the book of the living." And God is represented as declaring that He will bring His people home "that thy foot may be dipped in the blood of thine enemies, and the tongue of thy dogs in the same." Back of such words lies a conviction of the spotlessness of the speaker which entitles him to expect that his enemies shall be God's also. And yet all this violence has nothing in common with a steady confidence. These psalms repeat over and over descriptions of God's power to reassure the writer. Also they are designed to remind God that He is not making use of it. They try to arouse His pride:

Shall the enemy blaspheme thy name forever?
Arise, O God, plead thine own cause:
Remember how the foolish man reproacheth thee
    daily.
Forget not the voice of thine enemies. . . .
Wherefore should the heathen say, Where is their
    God?
Let him be known among the heathen in our sight
By the revenging of the blood of thy servants.

The men who prayed these prayers of fury had nothing to support them if God's vengeance was long delayed. They would wait a while, but then they would turn against Him. From other quarters, too, the old religion was in danger. The ideas in Deuteronomy could not satisfy this new world of bewildered pain.

One writer there was who never flinched before the logic of the argument drawn from experience against the justice of God, the author of the main part of the Book of Job. The conversations between Job and his three friends are generally held to belong to the Exile or soon after. They are based upon the early story of Job's patience when Satan afflicted him, but they are quite different in tone: Job is not patient at all, but bitterly resentful of his sufferings. They are equally different from the last part, a splendid hymn of praise to Power before which in the end Job abhors himself and repents in dust and ashes. The Job of the conversations has no respect for power. He brings terrible charges against God precisely on the ground of His omnipotence.

If this part of the book was in truth written in Chaldea, it shows with immense force to what men who had to think things through were brought when God's promises to save His people seemed to have come to nothing. It reads like a direct and bitter attack upon Deuteronomy. Job's three friends who come to sympathize with him in his misery talk to him in just the way the authors of Deuteronomy would have approved. They tell him that since he is wretched he must have sinned; being wretched above all others, he must have sinned more than they all. No one innocent dies in misery, they say. To be sure, man is born unto trouble as the sparks fly upward, yet the good man will certainly be protected by God: he shall come to his grave in a full age, like as a shock of corn cometh in in his season. They call upon him finally to consider the ways of God and his own feebleness and submit:

Shall a mortal man be more just than God?
A man more pure than his maker?
Behold, he putteth no trust in his servants,
And his angels he chargeth with folly.
How much more them that dwell in houses of clay,
Whose foundation is in the dust,
Who are crushed before the moth.

This is the old argument of power as worshipful in itself, which Deuteronomy took for granted. Job rejects it. He denies that man should reverence divine power no matter how it is exercised. The question turns on justice and in his own case God has not acted justly. He has done no wrong nor deserved in any way what has come upon him. He says sternly to God, "Thou knowest that I am not wicked." He asks Him, "Is it good unto thee that thou shouldst oppress?" No: the truth is that omnipotence belongs to God, but justice does not. "The guiltless and the innocent he destroys. . . . He would merely laugh at the death of the innocent." God does as He chooses and men are helpless. The stern conclusion is:

Let him slay me, I have no hope.
But mine integrity I will maintain in his very face.

Many a captive in Babylon must have come to the same blackness of despair: a merciless God, with no care for justice; man's Creator who yet would not have pity on the work of His own hand, so feeble as he knew it to be, and of so brief a span. For these men Job's words spoke the deepest searchings of their spirit. There was no hope, not here nor hereafter.

Thou hast made me as the clay. . . .
Wherefore didst thou bring me forth from the womb?

Let me alone that I may take comfort a little
Before I go whence I shall not return.
Even to the land of darkness, as darkness itself,
And of the shadow of death
Where the light is darkness.

A long road had been traveled away from the
comfortable man in Deuteronomy, dutifully keeping the commandments and contentedly secure in
his "houses full of all good things," his vineyards
and fields and live stock, his men servants and
maid servants. That ideal had ceased to be rele-
vant for the Hebrew nation. As a nation they were
never to be prosperous again. A God Whose re-
wards were prosperity could no longer meet their
needs. In the Exile they found another God. His
spokesman was the great poet we call the second
Isaiah because he wrote many of the last chapters
of that book and we do not know his name. During his life the Exile came to an end.

Babylon fell before the Medes and the Persians
in 539, just about fifty years after the fall of Jerusalem. As it is written in the Book of Daniel:
"Belshazzar the king made a great feast to a thousand of his lords. . . . At the same hour came
forth fingers of a man's hand and wrote upon the
plaister of the wall" three words in an unknown
language. A young Hebrew captive brought in
to interpret them said they meant, "Thou art
weighed in the balances, and art found wanting.

Thy kingdom is given to the Medes and Persians."
"In that night," the story continues, "was Belshaz-
zar king of the Chaldeans slain. And Darius, the
Median, took the kingdom."

To pass from Nebuchadnezzar to the Medes is
like leaving a dim, almost unknown world for one
familiar and clearly outlined. With the end of
Babylon the Greek world begins. Cyrus, the
leader of the Medes and Persians when they swept
over the East to the very shores of the Aegean
and when they conquered Chaldea, was a hero of
heroes to the Greeks. Herodotus told marvelous
stories about him; Xenophon held up a highly
idealized account of the way he was trained as a
model to parents and educators. His young general, Darius, according to the Bible story the
actual conqueror of Babylon, was the same man
who later received back a defeated army from the
field of Marathon.

The triumph of the Hebrews when the hated
city fell can be read in many a chapter of the Bible.
Another nameless poet who wrote one of the inter-
polated parts in the book of the first Isaiah, voices
it best of all:

> The burden of Babylon. . . .
> Behold I will stir up the Medes against them,
> Who shall not regard silver,
> And as for gold they shall not delight in it—

[a statement in exact agreement with what the Greeks said of them]

And Babylon, the glory of kingdoms . . .
Shall be as when God overthrew Sodom and Gomor-
    rah.
It shall never be inhabited. . . .
Neither shall the Arabian pitch tent there. . .
And the wild beasts of the desert shall lie there.
And the jackals shall cry in their desolate houses. . . .
Hell from beneath is moved for thee
To meet thee at thy coming. . . .
How art thou fallen from heaven,
O Lucifer, son of the morning!
As a carcase trodden underfoot.

During the century after the fall of Babylon, there is no contemporary Hebrew history. The books of Ezra and Nehemiah which give a description of the return to Jerusalem are now believed to have been written more than two centuries later. They follow the tradition that with the coming of Cyrus the nation's troubles ended. He set them free and promised them help if they wanted to go back and rebuild their city and temple. All the later allusions in the Bible bear this tradition out, as do also the contemporary passages about Cyrus in the second Isaiah: "I am the Lord . . . that saith of Cyrus, He is my shepherd, and shall perform all my pleasure: even saying to Jerusa-

lem, Thou shalt be built; and to the temple, Thy
foundation shall be laid. Thus saith the Lord to
his anointed, to Cyrus, whose right hand I have
holden to subdue nations before him. . . . He
shall build my city and he shall let go my captives." This surprising transformation of the great
Persian raider into God's anointed becomes natural when the people's rapture at the ending of
the Exile is taken into account. An ecstasy of joy
swept through them:

When the Lord turned again the captivity of Zion,
We were like them that dream.
Then was our mouth filled with laughter,
And our tongue with singing.
Then said they among the heathen,
The Lord hath done great things for them. . . .
They that sow in tears
Shall reap in joy.
He that goeth forth and weepeth, bearing precious
    seed,
Shall doubtless come again with rejoicing, bringing his
    sheaves with him.

The moment when Babylon fell and freedom
once more opened out before them was the most
exultant in Hebrew history, what Salamis was to
the Greeks and the destruction of the Armada to
the Elizabethans, but greatly transcending these
just as the sufferings before had been incompara-
bly greater. Such times create poets, Aeschylus

in Athens, Shakespeare in England, and for the Hebrews the poet known as the second Isaiah, the greatest poet in the Bible.

He is a new appearance there, not like anyone before him. He himself was perfectly aware that it was so; he realized that what he said was new. Over and over he repeats the word joyfully: "New things do I declare— Sing unto the Lord a new song— New heavens and a new earth." Like Christ and unlike theologians he did not think that which hath been said by them of old sufficed forever. He declared that God Himself said, "Remember ye not the former things. . . . Behold I will do a new thing." Indeed, his newness, the difference between him and the prophets before him, is startling. They thunder of God's vengeance; he sings of God's kindness. They see the world a place of black evil; he sees it full of gladness, the waste places breaking forth into joy. They look at mankind and find only cruelty and treachery and vileness; he looks at God, as infinite in mercy as in power, Who says to man, worm though he is, "I have blotted out as a thick cloud thy transgressions"; "I, even I, am he that comforteth thee"; "With everlasting kindness will I have mercy on thee."

In the first Isaiah the phrase oftenest repeated is, Woe unto them. So begin God's terrible threats to the wicked. Essentially, He says to them only,

"Fear me." "Fear and the pit are upon thee, O inhabitant of the earth." In the second Isaiah the words perpetually repeated are, "Fear not," and, extraordinarily, God, the awful God, is the reason why there is nothing to fear. His own words are: "Fear not, for I am with thee"; "For I the Lord thy God will hold thy right hand saying, Fear not. Thou shalt know that I the Lord am thy saviour." These would have been strange statements to Amos. But this new message which was to blot out the remembrance of the past had never been heard before in all the world; even Hosea had caught only part of it. The God of fear, the nameless poet declared, was ended. The Ancient of days, whose terror had darkened all the ages, had gone, and, in the poet's radiant vision, he would never return. No one any more afraid. A world free from fear. As the old Epicurean teacher wrote outside his cell, There is nothing to fear in God.

It is Hosea's deepest belief, worked out to its necessary conclusion, as Hosea was not able to do. Something, however, Hosea alone of all the prophets saw, that love and power belong in separate categories so that the exercise of the one is not compatible with the exercise of the other. This great idea is not to be found anywhere in the second Isaiah. All the poet sees is omnipotence grown compassionate—or, perhaps, it was always so:

Hast thou not known? hast thou not heard,
That the everlasting God, the Lord,
The Creator of the ends of the earth,
Fainteth not, neither is weary?
There is no searching of his understanding.
He giveth power to the faint;
And to them that have no might he increaseth strength.

.   .   .   .

With everlasting kindness will I have compassion upon
     thee,
Saith the Lord thy Redeemer.
For the mountains shall depart,
And the hills be removed;
But my kindness shall not depart from thee,
Saith the Lord that hath compassion upon thee.

Before the writer's absorption in this great conception what was of first importance to the men before him falls into the background. The case of
the poor recedes, along with attacks upon the rich.
Only once the old prophetic note is struck:

When the poor and needy seek water and there is none,
I, the Lord, will hear them.

Once too the wicked and the rich are classed
together. But these matters do not press upon him.
There is not a trace of the passion of anger that
swept through Amos and the first Isaiah at the
oppression of the weak. It may be that the suffering community of captives had been brought to-

gether by the sharing in a common pain. Perhaps
for once the bitter difference had ceased to be
bitter. Or it may be that, as has happened so often
to mystics enraptured by the beatific vision to the
point of losing sight of earthly things, he trusted
in all serenity of spirit the poor and the weak to
the God he saw so rapturously, the good Shepherd
Who carries the lambs in His bosom; the Redeemer Who brings them that sit in darkness out
of the prison house; Who opens the blind eyes
and blots out transgression. There he may have
found his perfect solution for all the wronged of
earth, his own release from the necessity the men
before him had been under to right those wrongs
themselves. Never an idea entered Amos' mind
that he could put off on God his own responsibility
for the poor. But to the second Isaiah the whole
question of poverty and oppression was unimpor-
tant. He was not concerned with it at all.

In the same way he dismissed the question of
ritual and righteousness which had so fired the
men before him. There are verses in these chapters which recall Ezekiel and would have aroused
the mighty wrath of Amos: the uncircumcised and
the unclean shall not enter the holy city; the
man who keeps the Sabbath from polluting it, is
blessed; God will accept burnt offerings and sacrifices upon His altar. Still, these are very occa-
sional passages and not to be greatly stressed in

view of the fact that it would be a pious act for later generations to add such sentiments to a book that seemed too chary of them and yet did not, like Amos, directly contradict them. Against the conclusion that the great poet really believed that only the circumcised were fit to enter Jerusalem is a statement that strangers who love the Lord will be made joyful in His house of prayer.

On the other hand, there is not one word against ritual. Nevertheless, it is impossible to think of him as standing for it, only as not caring one way or the other. It did not trouble him; he saw so clearly what lay behind it, the search through the visible for the invisible. The one passage unmistakably his which speaks of ritual, in this case sacrifice, has nothing whatever to do with ceremonies in temples:

Who hath directed the spirit of the Lord? . . .
Behold the nations are as a drop of a bucket,
And are counted as the small dust of the balance. . . .
And Lebanon is not sufficient to burn,
Nor the beasts thereof sufficient for a burnt offering.

Offer sacrifices or withhold them, he seems to say. Only be sure to see the importance of whichever you do in the true perspective.

Such things were side issues to him, nothing to spend time upon. Next to the tender love and compassion he found in God, joy and pain preoccupied

him, this joy at the ending of the Exile, that pain
of the Captivity. He saw them not as particular
experiences of the Hebrews, what they had felt
of homesick longing and misery in oppression, of
rapture at freedom and satisfied desire. He looked
at them *sub specie aeternitatis*—in their eternal
aspect, as poets do. Joy and pain seen in themselves, and seen as related, joy against a background of tears, conditioned by sorrow and known
only to the sorrowful. It was so radiant because
the background behind it was black. As the first
Isaiah had said,

The people that walked in darkness
Have seen a great light;
They that dwelt in the land of the shadow of death,
Upon them hath the light shined.

The mere ending of a sorrow could not call it
forth; it was not passive, but triumphant. It could
not come from simply receiving; it was an achievement, a conquest. To be set free from long-endur-
ing grief and consoled for the past meant seeing
the past from a loftier level, not easy of access:

Comfort ye, comfort ye my people, saith your God.
Speak ye comfortably to Jerusalem,
And cry unto her,
That her warfare is accomplished

.   .   .   .

Break forth into joy, sing together,
Ye waste places of Jerusalem.
For the Lord hath comforted his people. . . .
And everlasting joy shall be upon their head . . .
And sorrow and mourning shall flee away.

So, at last, the problem of evil, which is above all the problem of pain, ceased from troubling. He made no attempt to explain it as chastening from God to make a man better, in the way Deuteronomy had pointed out. To perceive in pain a means for self-improvement was farthest from his thought. He saw it as a means for enabling men to help each other. Only the suffering could help the sufferers of earth. A man of sorrows and acquainted with grief. Who else could speak to the giant agony of the world? In this light, the affliction of the innocent ceased to be impenetrable darkness.

The Jews understand the extraordinary fifty-third chapter of Isaiah (written, of course, by the second, not the first, Isaiah), that immortal picture of one who suffers for the good of others, as describing Israel's mission to give to the world what they have learned through their ages-long discipline of misery and anguish; the Christians see it as foretelling the mission of Christ. What is certain is that it expresses the beneficence of unselfish pain:

> He was wounded for our transgressions,
> He was bruised for our iniquities;
> The chastisement of our peace was upon him;
> And with his stripes we are healed.

As was the prophets' way, the writer did not explain. He did not reason out a philosophy of suffering, he showed one who suffered pain undeserved. He drew a picture of God afflicting the innocent, as Job had charged, and in face of it the idea of a God Who valued prosperity as His best gift shriveled to nothing. The God of the fifty-third and fifty-fifth chapters saw otherwise:

> It pleased the Lord to bruise him;
> He hath put him to grief . . .
> That the purpose of the Lord might prosper by his
>   hand. . . .
> .   .   .   .
> For my thoughts are not your thoughts,
> Neither are your ways my ways, saith the Lord.
> For as the heavens are higher than the earth,
> So are my ways higher than your ways,
> And my thoughts than your thoughts.

To suffer for others, the hardest part of the human lot, was not to be punished, but to help the purpose of the Lord to prosper. Pain was the other aspect of love, as God Himself knew Who suffered because He loved:

> In all their affliction he was afflicted.

St. Paul (or another) saw mankind surrounded by a great cloud of witnesses from whom, because they suffered and died, men drew patience to run the race set before them. Their happy prosperity would have meant nothing. Their pain and loss, by which alone any action can be proved to be disinterested, were the proof that in the mystery of evil lay the condition of the very highest good conceivable to mankind.

And though the Lord give you the bread of adversity, and the water of affliction, yet shall not thy teachers be removed into a corner any more, but thine eyes shall see thy teachers:

And thine ears shall hear a word behind thee, saying, This is the way, walk ye in it, when ye turn to the right hand, and when ye turn to the left.

Isaiah 30:20, 21

CHAPTER XII

The Prophets
of Israel

❖ ❖

THIS CHAPTER is not an attempt to sum-
marize all that the prophets thought, but
only what they thought which has value today.
Throughout their writings, as has been pointed
out, God keeps on rejoicing in the blood of His
enemies, although, indeed, less and less. But that
is a left-over from which they could not completely free themselves. It has no meaning now
except to the antiquarian and the historian. There
is no place for it in an appraisement of the prophets' achievement. What counts in their idea of
God is that they were the first to see that love and
compassion must belong to the divine. In what
follows nothing will be considered except the
truths they perceived as important which are still
important. The list is not a short one.

Practical wisdom, at once far-sighted and for present application, marked the prophets. Not practical, however, in the sense that the man who compromises is called practical, which is, indeed, like calling the near-sighted the clear-sighted. The prophets' vision was not faulty. They never urged accepting a little good at the price of a great good because it was nearer. That would have been an extravagant folly to them, the very reverse of the practical. Tested by the only test they ever admitted as valid—how a thing worked out to help men or to hinder them—the little good always broke down. The prophets never compromised. But their eyes were keen to see into basic problems of life. It would have been inconceivable to them all that religion was not directly concerned with everything that bore in any way on life; the whole of life belonged to religion. They all taught what is often called "pure religion," the dependence of the individual upon God, but it would never have occurred to them when they were urging the people to defy Assyria or submit to Babylon that they were talking politics and not religion. One reason for this point of view was that they did not think at all about fitting men for heaven, but only about fitting men to make the world a good place to live in. Politics upon this basis was everyone's plain religious duty. So, too, was economics. Problems of poverty and wealth are keenly analyzed in their writings. Amos is the ancestor of all labor agitators; in his book is the first recorded attack of labor upon capital.

Their practical bias is shown again in their complete disregard of that historical firebrand, theology. They never enunciated a creed or stated a dogma or essayed a definition of anything they believed. The only test of a man's religion to which they gave a thought was the way that man acted. Christ was so truly a son of the prophets that His words often illustrate their attitude, as in the story of the Good Samaritan when He made a priest and a Levite, types of strict theological orthodoxy, "pass by on the other side" from the man who had fallen among thieves, and chose a Samaritan, a heretic, to be "neighbor" to him: "But a certain Samaritan, as he journeyed, came where he was: and when he saw him, he had compassion on him." As if today an important bishop and a popular fundamentalist preacher should be condemned as compared with an agnostic scientist in a free clinic, or, since our dearest orthodoxies are economic rather than theological, a banker and an industrialist go down before a radical soap-box orator. There are verses in the prophets which would have a familiar ring if delivered from a soapbox: "The lofty city, the foot shall tread it down, even the feet of the poor and the steps of the needy."

Still, it is true that much of what the prophets

said belongs to their own day, not to ours. The politics they threw themselves into with such vehemence are comprehensible now only to the scholar. And when they said an earthquake happened because God had arisen to shake terribly the earth, they were offering their own scientific explanation which long since yielded to others as every explanation does. Old ideas are continually being slain by new facts. There is nothing stable in the conclusions of the mind, and it is impossible that there ever should be unless we hold that the universe is made to the measure of the human mind, an assumption for which nothing in the past gives any warrant.

Intellectually the prophets' world is not our world, but that fact does not touch their value to us. Spiritually they are our teachers. We have more information than they, that is all, and any sense of superiority based on such grounds is stultifying. We shall never know the truth if that is our attitude. Indeed, there is no foe so deadly to the truth as intellectual assurance. It substitutes an easy and shallow certainty for the deep loyalties of faith. It puts an end to thought, which can live only if it is free to change. Uncertainty is the prerequisite to gaining knowledge and frequently the result as well. Greater knowledge does not mean greater certainty. Oftenest the very reverse is true. We are certain in proportion as we do not know. We seem, indeed, so made that intellectual certainty is not good for us. We grow arrogant, intolerant, unable to learn and to attain to better grounds of certainty precisely because we are certain. The right attitude for the mind would seem to be humility.

But human experience does not change. Love and grief and joy remain forever the same. Beauty remains forever beautiful and poetic truth is always true. Complete security is possible for the spirit. What we experience we are sure of as of nothing else, and the sureness never bars the road to deeper experience. The certainty love knows does not stand in the way of greater love.

Truths of the spirit are true always. The greatest teachers of the Old Testament understood them as no men have more, and in their pages we can find ourselves. Our aspirations are there, our desires for humanity. They knew what lies deepest in men's hearts, and they gave it an expression so magnificent and so truthful, it still speaks for us today.

The prophets knew that they were spokesmen of God. They knew that they were as nothing before God's unutterable excellency and glory, and yet each one felt that he had come close to God. Each one had found out for himself the reality of the spiritual. In their day there was practically no second-hand experience to fall back on. They had no sacrosanct authority, Church or Book, to make their convictions for them. They were lonely men, who made their way to God alone. Each had a spiritual experience so actual, so vivid, it was like sight and sound, like the touch of a hand, like contact with a burning coal. The reality of it they proved in the only way any experience can be proved real, by the way they acted upon it.

The religion of the prophets has had an enduring influence in both the Jewish religion and the Christian religion, but not a decisive influence. The prophets did not direct the way either religion took. Their judgments of value were based entirely on how anything worked out to help bring about a good life for men. They rejected ritual because, far from being a help here, it was an obstacle; its tendency was always to become an easy substitute. They never entertained the idea of religion as an end in itself, comforting, satisfying aspiration toward inward purity and personal perfection. And they never said, Believe this and you shall live. Both of these ways also could so easily be made substitutes. Religion's way was different and not easy: Do this and you shall live. Upon God's true worshipers rested the tremendous responsibility of making God's will a reality upon the earth.

The greatness of the prophets consists first of

all in their conception of what His will was. They had a vision of what was possible for men, a vision at no time even approximately realized in the nearly three thousand years between them and us, yet so important for human life that it has never been dismissed. It has never been put in the category of the dream palaces men are always building to console themselves for things as they are. The prophets saw a world where no man was wronged by another, where the strong shared with the weak, where no individual was sacrificed for an end, where each individual was prepared to sacrifice himself for the end of making what God wished become a realized good.

We cannot dismiss this vision. The prophets show us what we know should be. The world they point us to cannot be given up as forever unattainable. We must feel that we are struggling toward it. Christ's conception was fundamentally the same: Thy will be done on earth.

With this idea of what God would have, they valued only the beliefs which resulted in definite good for life. Nevertheless none of them externalized religion into a set of good deeds, drawn up and written down for men to follow accurately. That way the good deeds would never be done, certainly not often or for long. They knew human nature. They wanted a different world but they knew the only way to get it was for men to be different. They never worked out a system or built up an organization—not until Ezekiel. Justice and mercy would prevail on the earth only if men wanted them.

There is a great deal in the prophets about punishing people into being good, but that again was left over from the old fear worship. Amos' words that justice must well up as waters and righteousness as a mighty stream show his clear perception that they would come to pass only when they were the free and spontaneous expression of the desire of men's hearts. This is the prophetic light at its brightest, and it is the light that counts, not the dark places it has not yet reached. There would be no end to the use of the poor by the rich, of the weak by the strong, until men wished to end it, from no calculation or constraint, but of themselves, through their own discovery of God, their own experience of the reality of the spiritual, their own vision of justice and mercy, and their own desire, which would result inevitably and irresistibly in making them actual, a realized good on earth. Then at last the prisoners and they that are in darkness would be brought out of the prison house of poverty and oppression.

In their day economic conditions were bad; the discrepancy between the rich and the poor was very wide and all the time growing wider. On all sides everywhere could be seen a few men using many men purely for their own advantage. This was the greatest evil in the world to Amos and the others, and therefore with their idea of religion it was the natural and inevitable field for religion. In such a condition of affairs religion would first of all be concerned with economics. They saw the matter very simply. All riches came from covetousness. A rich man was one who wanted more than his own share. He wanted other people's too and succeeded in getting it. This state of things was abhorrent to God and what He asked of His worshipers was to end it.

A fair pattern of life—a correct definition of "the substance" of the Father and "the substance" of the Son—neither of these roads was the way the prophets saw as the road to God. In their eyes men of religion were committed to a definite enterprise, to end all injustice, the core of which to them was economic injustice.

The prophets' way was not the way the Jewish religion went. Their way as reinforced by Christ was not the way the Christian religion went. A series of infinitely complicated acts, a series of infinitely complicated definitions, took the foremost place in the one and in the other. The ghettos were not marked out because in them the inequalities of wealth and poverty were leveled. The tremendous structure of what is called the Christian church did just what the priests of Deuteronomy had done, urged the bitter bread of charity as the only possible help for the poor.

In the prophets' day too there was the great structure of organized religion, so ancient and so splendid and so awe-inspiring with its suggestions of supernatural power. Amos and Hosea and Isaiah looked at it and they saw men building temples and offering sacrifices and profiting at the expense of others, bent only upon their own advantage and putting up a screen of worship between their consciences and their lives. They shook themselves free of it. They had their own knowledge of God. He was the God Who meeteth him that worketh righteousness. He could be known only when men judged the cause of the poor and the needy.

The prophets' sense of values was sure. They knew unerringly what was important and what was not. Religion's work was to create a world where no one was oppressed. There is not a trace in any of them of the idea that the way to do God's will was to seek for personal holiness. Amos, Micah, Isaiah, Ezekiel too, have not left a word to show that they ever thought about themselves at all. Jeremiah has. He gives us some account of his inner life, of his prayers and how God answered them, but it is singularly unlike all other records of saintly communion with the Lord. There is not a petition about his own improvement; there is no spiritual exaltation. His prayers, for the most part, are like a conference with God. He puts his puzzles before Him, why the wicked prosper and the prophets lie; one very long prayer is about his purchase of a farm. The tone is that of a man who is seeking to understand the world and what he is to do about it. He asks the Lord for information and for guidance, and the answer is invariably to go and do something the Lord wants done. There is not a touch of ecstasy in one of these prayers. They move in the opposite direction to prayer as usually understood, away from the world of the soul to the world outside. The other prophets leave their prayers out and give only what God says, except for that briefest prayer of Isaiah: "Here am I, send me."

They could not but feel this way about prayer with their sense of the overwhelming importance of creating a good life for men here on earth. No one ever saw the task as harder than they did; no one ever saw evil more clearly and felt a deeper rejection of it. But they never turned away to think of a world to come where evil could not enter; it never entered their minds to rise above this evil world by despising it and seek their own salvation in an ecstasy of faith. They were convinced beyond everything else of the reality of the spiritual and its supreme importance, but they kept their feet always on the ground, their eyes always on human life, their interest directed only to improve it, never themselves. They felt no contempt for the world. It was God's; He had a purpose for it; and their part was to help to carry it out.

They never had a doubt that God's will could not be brought to pass in any other way. It is curious that with their complete belief in His omnipotence, their majestic conception of what He was, the everlasting God, the Lord, the Creator of the ends of the earth, and their profound conviction of men's weakness and wickedness, they were nevertheless sure that He could not do without them. The human heart was deceitful above all things and desperately wicked; man was a leaf that withered and was blown away, and yet he and he alone could bring about the will of God; to do so was the obligation God laid upon him.

It is true that they all talk perpetually about what God is going to bring to pass, whether of evil to punish the wicked, or of good, to establish His kingdom on earth, but when their words are read with care it becomes clear that except for storms and earthquakes and the like, what God does to men is done by men. The Assyrian is the rod of His anger; He will stir up the Medes to punish the wickedness of Babylon; Nebuchadnezzar is His tool and so is Cyrus. There is a spirit of energy throughout, no idea of watching God work. God expects men to work for Him. Jeremiah with his passionate conviction that God was "the God of all flesh for whom nothing is too hard" never for a moment thought that he could withdraw, give himself up to prayer, for instance, and leave the issue to God. He knew that he had to be God's spokesman. That was the only way God could speak to Jerusalem.

When in the temple Isaiah heard God say: "Go and tell this people," he knew the responsibility was his. Convinced that he had seen God attended by awful beings, mysterious servants of the Most High, it never occurred to him that one of them would be a more convincing bearer of God's message. He knew more than he was consciously aware of. Believing with his whole heart in God's omnipotent power, he knew nevertheless that a demonstration of that power in some marvelous way could do nothing to forward his own work, the work God had put upon him, to turn men from wanting evil to wanting good.

There are no marvels in the prophets. They never worked miracles. At the end of the first Isaiah there is a story about his convincing Hezekiah by making the shadow on the sundial go back, but it is a late addition. Isaiah never stood on that level. He did indeed believe Sennacherib's retreat to be an act of God in favor of Jerusalem, but there he was trying to explain a notably strange event. To reverse the shadow on the sundial is a matter of an altogether different order. It bears the hall-mark of magic; it is an exhibition of inexplicable power to compel belief. Nothing else in the proph-ets has any remote connection with that sort of thing.

They all knew that the cause they were fight-ing for could not be helped in that way. The sight of the sun retracing his course at noonday would not do anything toward bringing the spirit of jus-tice and mercy to men.

If the sun went backward that would be a fact independent of men. They could not make it more real or less real. They could watch it and reason about it, but they could not affect it. But the truth the prophets were concerned with was dependent on men. Justice, mercy, all the truths of the spirit, could not be grasped by looking at them or think-ing about them but only by acting upon them, by living them. Love, the central truth of the spirit, cannot be understood by the observation of the mind or by the perception of its spiritual beauty. It must be experienced; it will never be known otherwise. Nor can its presence be proved intel-lectually, or in any way except by living it. It is an experience of which the proof is unselfish ac-tion. If men became wholly selfish they would prove irrefutably that there was no love among them.

Justice and mercy—where will they be if men do not show them? Their truth, their reality on earth, depends upon the way men act. If men fail to be just and merciful there will be no justice and mercy.

Galileo's recantation has done him no harm in the esteem of mankind. He acted sensibly in refusing to be tortured or killed for the sake of the world's moving around the sun. That fact was completely independent of him. It did not need his support. He could withdraw it in all tranquillity of spirit and as he left the inquisition chamber toss back over his shoulder the gibing, "All the same, it does move," with no sense of betrayal. Who would be a martyr in order to maintain that the square described on the hypotenuse of a right-angled triangle is equal to the sum of the squares described on the two other sides? How would martyrdom help prove it?

But the truths of the spirit can be proved only by what we do about them. "Love, joy, peace, long-suffering, gentleness, goodness, faith"—if we should cease to show them in our lives, they would cease to be. Apart from us they have no existence here. There is no way to prove that there is disinterestedness except by being disinterested.

To act so that these words may be true—that

is the logic of the spirit. An ideal is not a utopian dream, it is a goal; however remote, it can be reached. In some sort, it can be made real by every man—by living it or dying for it.

The prophets' ideal was conceived with the utmost simplicity and directness in terms of actual life. Men could bring it to pass; it was a goal they could attain to. "And they shall beat their swords into plowshares and their spears into pruning hooks; nation shall not lift up sword against nation, neither shall they learn war any more, and none shall make them afraid." Through such words men catch a glimpse of a world they must try to create. Not centuries, but millennia, have passed since those words were written, and yet they do not bring a sense of hopelessness that as they never have been made true, so they never will be. Fire is in them forever to kindle the desire that they shall be true. The excellent becomes the permanent, said the Greeks. When mankind have seen a good, they do not ever let it go. They are not able, as human beings it is not in them, to blot it out completely and forget it. What the prophets wanted for the world has never been dropped from men's consciousness. The possibilities they discovered we still must strive to realize. The desires of the best and greatest have a strange authority; they carry compulsion.

Thou wilt light my candle: The Lord my God will enlighten my darkness.

Psalms 18:28

The spirit of man is the candle of the Lord.

Proverbs 20:27

CHAPTER XIII

The
Sunlit Heights

❖ ❖ ❖ ❖ ❖ ❖ ❖ ❖ ❖ ❖ ❖ ❖ ❖ ❖ ❖ ❖ ❖ ❖ ❖

THE TRUE nature of anything, Aristotle says, is what it becomes at its highest. Nothing shows this more clearly than the Old Testament. Its true nature is a conception of God which has never been transcended for greatness and elevation and beauty, and a knowledge as profound as there has ever been of man's weakness and wickedness and power to find God. This is the teaching of the Old Testament at its loftiest, and nothing which is on a lower level is important for religion. In what follows only the heights are considered.

"And, behold, a great and strong wind rent the mountains, and broke in pieces the rocks; but the Lord was not in the wind: and after the wind an earthquake; but the Lord was not in the earthquake: and after the earthquake a fire, but the Lord was not in the fire: and after the fire a still small voice. And it was so, when Elijah heard it, that he wrapped his face in his mantle, and went out, and stood in the entering in of the cave. And behold, there came a voice unto him and said, What doest thou here, Elijah?"

We cannot date this passage. It is in the Book of Kings, in which often the older and the later parts cannot be definitely distinguished. That is a great pity as regards this particular part, for there is not a more remarkable passage in the Old Testament.

The God of Moses was in the fire. He revealed Himself in a burning bush. He descended to Mount Sinai "in fire, and the smoke thereof ascended as the smoke of a furnace." To many a psalmist He was in the wind: "He did fly upon the wings of the wind"; "The voice of the Lord . . . breaketh the cedars of Lebanon"; "Stormy wind fulfilling His word." He was in the earthquake: "The earth shook and trembled, the foundations also of the hills moved because he was wroth." The God manifested in physical power is often met with in the Bible from the earliest times to the loftiest of the prophets. But countering this idea is another, phrased for the first time, quite possibly, in this story of Elijah,

and coming more and more to the fore, of One
Who did indeed lay the foundations of the earth
and Who keeps the stars in their courses, but
Whose voice is the still small voice within, a
power beside which storm and earthquake and
fire are as nothing.

The Old Testament is used today as an authority for God, as a proof that God is and a proof of
what He is. Since Isaiah says this or that, God
is this or that. But in the Old Testament that line
of reasoning is absent. Moses is the greatest of
the Hebrews and we are told that God talked with
him face to face, but neither Isaiah nor anyone
else ever quoted the words God spoke to him to
support his own belief in God. The Psalms do
not say, "Know that all the gods of the nations
are idols: but the Lord made the heavens, for
Moses declared that it is so." Isaiah never told
his fellow exiles, "Moses said God is a merciful
God, therefore be sure that he will abundantly
pardon." Both Jeremiah and Ezekiel had described God as the good shepherd—Isaiah, too
—but the author of the 23d Psalm felt no need
to go back to these great teachers for this authority
when he said, "The Lord is my shepherd." He had
his own knowledge. In Hosea and the second
Isaiah there were beautiful, tender sayings about
the love of God, but the man who wrote the 103d
Psalm did not bring forward any of them to

strengthen his own assertion, "Bless the Lord, O my soul, who crowneth thee with loving kindness and tender mercies." He expressed what he himself had learned and knew was true because he had learned it from God.

Every one of the great teachers of the Old Testament believed that he was in immediate contact with God. They knew even more than that. They believed that "the road to God is in the soul of every man." It was Athanasius who said that, but hundreds of years before, the Hebrews had said it. Man's spirit is the candle of God. God lights it—"The true light," St. John said, "which lighteth every man that cometh into the world"—and the still small voice speaks to all.

The Old Testament is the record of men's conviction that God speaks directly to men.

In the greatest Psalms, and especially in the Prophets, God is immeasurably, inconceivably, above His creation, infinite and eternal, not to be bounded by space and time: "For a thousand years in thy sight are but as yesterday when it is past"; "Behold, the heaven of heavens cannot contain thee." Against God's enduring faithfulness, "Even from everlasting to everlasting thou art God," is set man's feeble instability, "like the troubled sea, when it cannot rest." Man's vileness, "deceitful above all things and desperately wicked," is set against God's perfection Who is

worshiped in "the beauty of holiness." Nevertheless, in spite of this illimitable distance between
human and divine, God is "a God at hand." There
is a bond between Creator and created. "So God
created man in his own image." The two are not
separated by an impassable gulf. God is near, in-
timately near, to man.

> O Lord, Thou hast searched me,
>   and known me.
> Thou knowest my downsitting and
>   mine uprising,
> Thou understandest my thought
>   afar off. . . .
>
> For there is not a word in my
>   tongue,
> But, lo, O Lord, Thou knowest it
>   altogether.
>
> .   .   .   .
>
> Whither shall I go from Thy spirit?
> Or whither shall I flee from Thy
>   presence?
> If I ascend up into heaven, Thou
>   art there;
> If I make my bed in hell,
> Behold, Thou art there.
> If I take the wings of the morning,
> And dwell in the uttermost parts
>   of the sea;
> Even there shall Thy hand lead
>   me,
> And Thy right hand shall hold me.

The Old Testament has its own version of the great conception of the Incarnation, the Holy Spirit within the spirit of man. God is "the Beyond that is within":

> For thus saith the High and Lofty
> One
> That inhabiteth eternity, whose
> name is Holy:
> I dwell in the high and holy place,
> With him also that is of a contrite
> and humble spirit.

But to be brought near to God is to feel the awe of infinite perfection and an overwhelming sense of weakness and unworthiness. The radiancy of the divine light shows "the darkness where the light is as darkness" within men's hearts. "Thou hast set our iniquities before us, our secret sins in the light of thy countenance." There all is seen; nothing can be dimmed and made to look less black. "I acknowledge mine iniquity and my sin is ever before me."

This state of despairing self-knowledge is only briefly noted in the Old Testament. It is quickly succeeded by the enraptured knowledge of God. His light that shows men what they are shows too what He is. Perfect goodness is His, and therefore He is all-compassionate. He is "plenteous in mercy"; He will "abundantly pardon"; "For I the

Lord thy God will hold thy right hand, saying unto thee, Fear not; I will help thee." The soul says to Him, "If thou, Lord, shouldest mark iniquity, Lord, who would stand?" And God answers, "I have blotted out thy transgressions as a thick cloud, and as a cloud thy sins. Therefore return unto me for I have redeemed thee." A plenitude of merciful goodness, unbought by penitence and prayer, even unsought.

The assurance of free forgiveness undeserved brings an amazement of gratitude and joy. The soul is turned wholly to God, forgetting self, even self-reproach. "He inclined unto me and heard my cry. He brought me up also out of an horrible pit, out of the miry clay, and set my feet upon a rock. . . . And he hath put a new song in my mouth, even praise unto our God." "Oh that men would praise the Lord for his goodness and for his wonderful works to the children of men." "For he satisfieth the longing soul and filleth the hungry soul with goodness."

With this joy, this vision of the wonder of God, other wishes fade and there is left the single desire to draw nearer to the source of all good, to partake humbly of that good, for "clean hands and a pure heart," for "truth in the inward parts," as if there were nothing now in the world except the still small voice and the listening soul, which knows at last through God what is the will of God. "O thou

that hearest prayer, unto thee shall all flesh come."
Of all prayers ever uttered the most searching is,
"May the words of my mouth and the meditation
of my heart be acceptable in thy sight, O Lord,
my strength and my redeemer."

The end of the soul's progress in the Old Testament is, "Whom have I in heaven but thee? and
there is none upon earth that I desire beside thee."

Only the outside of life changes. Within, the
thing that hath been is that which shall be, and
there is no new thing under the sun. The Old
Testament is the great book of human experience,
and the greatest experience in it is in the Psalms
and the Prophets. They had profound knowledge
of the matter fundamental to all knowledge: they
"knew what was in man." Their words do not
startle us with a sense of something strange and
new; they startle us with the revelation of a community of feeling, a similarity of outlook, between
us and that distant antiquity. They discover to us
what was always in us although we had not known
it. They are spokesmen for humanity. We realize
through them not only the permanence of every
great vision for the good, but the continuity of
human life, the underlying unity of human beings.
Life looked the same to them as it does to us, so
brief for all its strange unbroken flow, with birth
forever following upon death. They saw it as we

do and before its mystery they felt the same sharp pang of pain.

This realization of how unchanging human experience is does not bring a sense of discouragement as lack of progress along other lines does. On the contrary, it is fortifying. Because all those before us have died, death is easier to face. They suffered and endured to create a better world, and in some strange way we are constrained to do the same. Because we are compassed about by so great a cloud of witnesses we can run with patience the race set before us.